Devotions
for
Nibblers

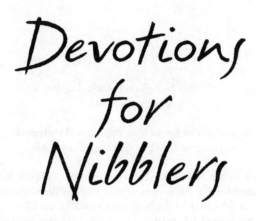

Devotions
for
Nibblers

KRISTEN JOHNSON INGRAM

CrossAmerica Books

CROSSINGS BOOK CLUB, GARDEN CITY, NEW YORK

CrossAmerica Books is an imprint and trademark
pending on behalf of Crossings Book Club.

Scripture quotations used in this book are from the New Revised
Standard Version Bible, copyright © 1989 by the Division of
Christian Education of the National Council of the Churches of
Christ in the USA, used by permission, all rights reserved.

Cover design by Sherry Sumerlin
Interior design by Debbie Glasserman

ISBN: 0-7394-3504-3

Printed in the United States of America

Devotions
for
Nibblers

Trusting God

He rained down on them manna to eat, and gave them the grain of heaven. Mortals ate of the bread of angels; he sent them food in abundance.

—Psalm 78:24, 25

I know God will supply what I need—but that isn't ever enough for me. I want more. I overeat, or I eat the wrong things, or both, and I think God wants me to look at what that behavior means.

I'm like one of the children of Israel in the wilderness. God sends me manna and I ask for meat; God sends meat, and I want a banana split. And at the core of all this asking and wanting is the mysterious fear that somehow I won't have enough—so I eat as much as I can whenever food is around.

Manna was good for only one day; you couldn't stock up on it because it spoiled. I think God is showing me that I'm saving my manna as body fat, which is spoiling my health, my appearance, and my dignity. What I have to do now is really believe that God wants the best for me.

FOR FURTHER REFLECTION

1. *Are you willing to let God satisfy your needs today?*
2. *Do you trust God to guide you about food?*
3. *Can you remember to gather God's love anew each morning, and not try to store it up?*

PRAYER

God, I need to believe You will take care of my relationship with food. Teach me real trust. Amen

Trojan Horse

Many seek the favor of the generous, and everyone is a friend to a giver of gifts.

—Proverbs 19:6

The ancient Greeks rolled a huge horse up to the gates of Troy as a symbol of defeat. You've beaten us, the gesture said, and we're offering you this wonderful horse to show we honor your gods. Then the Greeks hit. When the Trojans brought the gift inside the city walls, they discovered too late that it was full of Greek warriors. The city was destroyed.

Every day I get a different offer in the mail: free coffee beans, a free vacation. But just about every one of these "gifts" is a Trojan Horse. In fine print, I discover that I have to keep ordering coffee, or promise to drive to a remote location (at my own expense), then spend much of the "vacation" listening with a crowd of other travelers to time-share pitches.

Television ads keep offering me the gift of easy weight loss: I don't have to exercise and can eat all my favorite foods while the pounds melt away. And inside this enticing Trojan Horse are expensive (and usually worthless) products or dangerous herbs and drugs that could shoot my blood pressure sky high. There ain't no free horse.

FOR FURTHER REFLECTION

1. *Are you looking for an easy solution to your overeating problem?*
2. *Do you find yourself being gullible about free offers?*
3. *Are you willing to stop nibbling the harder way?*

PRAYER

Dear Lord, You've shown me that the only free gift is Your grace. Keep me alert to falsehood. Amen

The Race

I have fought the good fight, I have finished the race,
I have kept the faith.

—2 Timothy 4:7

When I was in high school and college, I ran the mile on our track teams. I was fast; I often broke the tape and won the race, but that was always a surprise. I never knew who was behind me or who was in front: I just ran my own race, listening to that tick-tock in my head that we call *pace*. I've learned since then that people who watch their competition or look over their shoulders do worse as runners.

But it's hard, when you're trying to lose weight or control your eating, *not* to watch other people, not to compare your progress with theirs. Jennifer, in my aerobics class, has lost twelve pounds—but I feel better when Laurie tells me she's lost only two. Elyse, my church friend, has gone for three weeks without butter or sugar, and I can't measure up. But Lenore confesses that she ate a whole carton of butter brickle ice cream, and then I breathe more easily.

My effort to stop nibbling isn't a competition. I've got to run my own race and be thankful when I break the tape at the end.

FOR FURTHER REFLECTION

1. *Are you competing with others as you try to stop overeating?*
2. *Does the success and failure of others affect the way you feel about yourself?*
3. *If so, how do you plan to deal with this?*

PRAYER

Help me to run my own race, dear God. Amen

Listening to My Body

And now, my children, listen to me:
happy are those who keep my ways.
Hear instruction and be wise, and do not neglect it.

—Proverbs 8:32, 33

Science has now mapped human genes, and I'm awed to know that when I was only a single cell, God had already put my DNA together, with instructions for my life. My body *knows* what it needs, has known since before I was born.

God didn't program me to eat more than I need. But my body and my appetite are now out of touch. My stomach *isn't* always asking for food, but I keep reaching for potato chips and chocolate chip cookies. I quench my thirst with soda pop, even though our city has some of the best water in the country. And when the brain God gave me asks for mental stimulation, I anesthetize it with food. I can listen to the body God gave me. And I can give my brain the food it needs: books, music, friends, and work.

FOR FURTHER REFLECTION

1. *What is your body telling you about your eating habits?*
2. *Even if you're overweight, could you be starved for vitamins and minerals?*
3. *How can you satisfy your creative urges without food?*

PRAYER

O God, You made me with a mind and body that know
what to do. Help me to listen to them. Amen

Movie Night

*No testing has overtaken you that is not common to everyone.
God is faithful, and he will not let you be tested beyond your
strength, but with the testing he will also provide the way out so
that you may be able to endure it.*

—1 Corinthians 10:13

I've thought since childhood that no matter how recently I've eaten beforehand, I have to munch, crunch, and gulp my way through a movie. Candy bars, popcorn, soft drinks—sometimes even a hot dog! But tonight, I tucked a bottle of spring water into my bag and we headed for the multiplex theater.

I kept my water bottle handy, and sipped on it several times during what turned out to be a wonderful movie. I saw people carrying giant-sized boxes of popcorn that smelled wonderful—but like coffee, I think popcorn smells better than it actually tastes. A couple of times I thought about those boxes of chocolate mints, and the super-sized cola drinks, but I got through the two hours without eating anything. And when we got out of the show, I realized I was actually still full from the supper we'd eaten just before we left.

This was a small but important victory. I have freed myself from one major nibbling occasion: movie night.

FOR FURTHER REFLECTION

1. *What occasions trigger your nibbling?*
2. *When did this pattern originate?*
3. *How will you change this model?*

PRAYER

*Thank You, God, for even the smallest victories in my battle
with overeating. Amen*

A Severe Mercy

No one who conceals transgressions will prosper,
but one who confesses and forsakes them will obtain mercy.
—Proverbs 28:13

My friend Debbie prayed for help losing weight, but, according to her, she wasn't doing much on her own. Then her car broke down, and the repair-shop owner didn't find an engine for five weeks. Debbie had to walk more than a mile to the bus stop. And because she couldn't drive through the fast-food places for lunch, she started taking a salad and fruit to work.

By the time her car was ready, she had lost ten pounds, and her waistline was an inch slimmer. Then, she says, she realized that through God's mercy—a severe, hard mercy—her prayer had been answered. God had made it possible for her to lose weight, and had shown her how to continue. Debbie resumed driving her car to work, but she took a long walk every morning and evening, and continued to eat a simple, healthy lunch. Soon she was at her goal weight and healthier than she had been for years.

Even a broken car can show God's love.

FOR FURTHER REFLECTION

Today, look for God's action in small inconveniences. Try to see the mechanic who can't fix your car right away as an angel from heaven, and the broken elevator that makes you walk upstairs as a mercy from God.

PRAYER

Dear Lord, I know You care for me and You are always acting for my good. Amen

Abandoned Cat

My master left me behind because I fell sick three days ago.
—1 Samuel 30:13

After her husband died, my neighbor was bitter that her husband hadn't left an estate. She let beautiful landscaping turn to weeds. Rather than selling the home they'd put so much money into, she allowed the mortgage company to foreclose. And when she got a job and moved to an apartment, she abandoned her beautiful, well-cared-for house cat.

A special animal shelter in our city specializes in cats. Rather than euthanizing, they work hard at finding homes, and keep cats too old for adoption as permanent guests. But although the kitty hangs around our porch, eats the food we put out, and has even ventured inside, we can't pick her up to take her to the shelter. She's so scared she bites, and bites hard, drawing blood.

I wonder if that's how I react to help from family or friends, especially about my eating. I may even have bitten God a time or two. Now it's time to take whatever assistance comes along.

FOR FURTHER REFLECTION

1. *Have your life experiences made you feel abandoned?*
2. *When others offer you help, do you "bite"?*
3. *Are you ready to let someone give you the help of counsel and advice?*

PRAYER

Dear God, I can be scared and defensive sometimes, like an abandoned cat. Teach me how to trust. Amen

A Different Kind of Hunger

Let them thank the Lord. For he satisfies the thirsty,
and the hungry he fills with good things.
—Psalm 107:8, 9

Recently I saw Norman Rockwell's painting *Freedom from Want.* It reminded me that the world is full of people starving for all kinds of things.

I'm starving for something I've thought was unreachable. I try to satisfy my inner longings with food when what I really want is love, or appreciation, or independence, or maybe even fame. And I don't know how to get those things. I'm not even sure how to pray for them.

But today, with God's help, I'm going to make one move toward one of my desires: I'll start to write that poem, or tell someone I need them, or make the phone call that will start me toward my goal. And if tomorrow I eat instead, I won't hate myself; I'll just pray again and try once more to achieve freedom from want.

FOR FURTHER REFLECTION

Write down some of the things you long for, and decide what small move you can make toward achieving one of them. When you make that move, check that item off and decide on another. Keep this list current.

PRAYER

Heavenly Father, help me to identify what I really want, and teach me how to reach for it. Amen

Guilty Eating

But if you refrain from vowing, you will not incur guilt.
—Deuteronomy 23:22

Just about every night I tell myself and God that the next day, I won't nibble between meals or eat the wrong things. But sometime during that next afternoon my hunger-light goes on and I start sneaking crackers with peanut butter, or cookies, or slices of cheese that get bigger each time.

When I say "sneaking" I don't mean I'm hiding from anyone. Nobody's there to see what I do. But I eat with a stealthy, guilty attitude because of my vow the previous evening. And the guiltier I feel, the more inclined I am to keep eating. For comfort's sake.

I fail at a lot of little pledges: *This weekend I'll clean out all the closets; tomorrow I'll begin studying a foreign language; next week I'll start scrimping and saving for a trip to France . . .*

The Bible says if you don't vow, you don't sin by failing. I think I set so many lofty goals for myself that I can't function when it comes to small ones, like taking my vitamins every day or skipping those afternoon snacks. I've got to sort out *attainable* goals and then take the first step toward them.

FOR FURTHER REFLECTION

1. *Do you constantly promise yourself that you'll do the unrealistic?*
2. *Is one of those vows connected to eating?*
3. *Would it help you to live "vow free"?*

PRAYER

Lord Jesus, You came to take away our guilt.
Help me to stop vowing the unrealistic so I won't always feel like I'm falling short. Amen

Nurturing

He will feed his flock like a shepherd; he will gather the lambs
in his arms, and carry them in his bosom,
and gently lead the mother sheep.

—Isaiah 40:11

The hardest thing for me to believe is that God cares for me, loves me like an only child. I keep thinking I have to earn God's approval, or live a sinless life. No matter how well I understand God's grace with my intellect, deep within me is the feeling that love and grace are for others, not me.

I don't know why I feel this way. I had a happy childhood with affectionate parents, but the little girl inside me believes she doesn't measure up. And that little girl *eats* to feel better.

I'm going to tell God about that little girl, and ask Him to nurture her the way mothers care for their children. And then maybe I can find something besides food to make me happy.

FOR FURTHER REFLECTION

1. *Do you really believe God loves and cares for you?*
2. *Are you eating so you'll feel better about yourself?*
3. *Are you willing to tell God how you feel?*

PRAYER

Dear Lord, the Bible and the Church say that You love me.
Teach me to be satisfied with Your love instead of food. Amen

The Wind's Song

I grew up in an Arizona mining town bordered on the east by
Apache Leap, a range of pink granite pinnacles that lifted into the
sky like a rosy crown. And in the wintertime, those mountains
sang. Cold air snaked between those pink pinnacles, and when it
emerged, the wind sang like a pipe organ.

I've been satisfying my mouth and stomach recently, but
remembering that mountain music, I realize the rest of my senses
are hungry. This evening, instead of sinking in front of the
television with a plate full of cookies, I think I'll feast my eyes and
ears and heart. I'll sit on the porch and listen for the song God
gives the wind as it dances through the tall fir trees behind my
house.

FOR FURTHER REFLECTION

*Today, find some beauty in the world around you, and take time to
relish that instead of too much food.*

PRAYER

*O God, You have made creation beautiful. Teach me how to see,
hear, and taste it, and to appreciate its fragrance. Amen*

Deprivation

*Happier were those pierced by the sword than those
pierced by hunger, whose life drains away, deprived
of the produce of the field.*

—Lamentations 4:9

I was scarfing down pizza as fast as I could. I'd been on three planes that day, without any lunch or dinner, and now, at almost ten o'clock, I was famished. My grandson watched me for a few minutes and said, chuckling, "Grandmother, you eat like a velociraptor."

"Hey, I'm hungry. I was deprived all day," I answered, pushing the last bite into my mouth. Of course, my idea of deprivation wouldn't stand up where people are really desperate for food. I'd eaten breakfast that morning, and each of the airlines had bestowed on me a package of pretzels.

I say I'm starving when I mean I want lunch, famished when dinner is an hour late, and deprived when I've had to skip a meal. Am I just being dramatic, or am I unconsciously scaring myself into overeating? Obviously, I need to revise my eating vocabulary. Otherwise I might turn into a velociraptor.

FOR FURTHER REFLECTION

1. *What words do you use to talk about being hungry?*
2. *How can you change the way you talk about food?*
3. *Besides food, what do you feel deprived of in your life?*

PRAYER

*Jesus, when You were on the cross, You said simply, "I thirst."
Help me to be less dramatic and more like You. Amen*

Justice

Is not this the fast that I choose: to loose the bonds of injustice . . .
Is it not to share your bread with the hungry, and bring the
homeless poor into your house?

—Isaiah 58:6, 7

As I was leaving the supermarket I encountered a young man with a sign that said he would work for food. I gave him a dollar and went on my way; I was hungry and rushed and I wanted the man out of my sight and mind. But as I loaded my groceries into the car, the word "justice" rang in my head.

In the majority of Bible translations, the word "charity" is not found in the Old Testament. Instead, the Law and the Prophets speak of *justice* to the poor. God said it is unjust for us to have so much we overeat, while any of His children are hungry.

I went back into the store and bought cheese, crackers, a packet of raw veggies, a jug of fruit juice, and some paper cups. I took the food out to the young man and we ate the cheese and crackers together and drank some juice, sitting on the dog food sacks outside the store.

Odd. I wasn't really hungry for the rest of that day.

FOR FURTHER REFLECTION

How many ways can you show God's justice to the hungry, the homeless, and the poor? And how will doing that affect your attitude toward food?

PRAYER

I want to bring Your kind of justice to the earth, God.
Give me the strength to try. Amen

Watching for a Sign

Others, to test him, kept demanding from him
a sign from heaven.

—Luke 11:16

As we sipped our tea, my friend said, "If I'm really supposed to lose weight, why doesn't God give me a sign?"

God probably *has* given her a sign. At her last checkup, her blood pressure was high and she was found to be hovering at the edge of diabetes. God was surely speaking through her test results.

Maybe our first sign from God comes when we can't button up our jeans or when we look awful in a favorite dress. Most of us don't see those events as heavenly messages, because we think God has to speak through the thunder, or send down some handwriting on the wall. The trick is recognizing signs in everyday things and events, and remembering that God is always nearby, always sending words of encouragement and direction.

FOR FURTHER REFLECTION

On a journal page, list the ways God has already shown you that you need to examine your relationship with food. Then list the ways you plan to respond to God's signs.

PRAYER

Open my eyes and ears, my God, so that I may see what You hold in store for me. Amen

Wishing on a Star

They served their idols, which became a snare to them.
—Psalm 106:36

At around age five, I recited the same list every evening when I saw the first star: *a rabbit, a horse, and a bicycle.* When I was old enough, I got the horse and the bike; my parents talked me out of the rabbit and bought me a wonderful dog instead. None of these gifts came because I asked a star, but because I also asked my parents! Wishing on stars is fun, but it's superstitious.

I've got to admit some superstitious attitudes about eating. Deep down, I think if I wish hard enough or think the right thoughts or pray "just right," using a formula that God likes, I'll miraculously quit overeating. In fact, I might even wake up thin. (And who knows? Maybe even ten years younger!)

But wishing and thinking and clever prayers aren't the answer. I don't need to ask a star; I need to ask God. I'll pray for enough strength to keep going in my fight against overeating.

FOR FURTHER REFLECTION

Sometimes superstition hides behind what you think is fact. Today, make a list of any strong opinions you have about food, eating, or methods of weight loss; then check to see which of these is really superstition. Then check the way you pray.

PRAYER

Almighty God, help me to quit wishing and start acting. Amen

Eating Without Hunger

He has filled the hungry with good things,
and sent the rich away empty.

—Luke 1:53

Ten o'clock: time for a "coffee break," which means Danish and a cola. Noon is the lunch hour. Maybe I'll have a cheeseburger and a malt. Two-thirty: another break, this time for cookies and tea with honey. Six o'clock, and dinner is on the table, and this time it's baked ham and chocolate cake for dessert. Bedtime at last, and a quick raid on the refrigerator.

I had some trouble swallowing that last forkful of chocolate cake, and my midnight snack—like all those eating events—was just a matter of habit.

But that day is past, and I'm looking at a new day. For my coffee break, a walk around the block. At lunch time, I'm going to walk *ten* blocks to a deli where I can get a nice salad. This afternoon, instead of eating, I'm going to help my scared new co-worker learn to use our temperamental copy machine. And throughout the day I'm going to keep reaching for the water and some raw vegetables instead of an unnecessary and unhealthy snack. Maybe by dinnertime, I'll actually be hungry for a change.

FOR FURTHER REFLECTION

1. How many times a day do you eat?
2. How many of those times are you really hungry?
3. How can you change that pattern?

PRAYER

Lord, I could find enough food in my cupboards to last a month.
Teach me to eat it only when I'm hungry. Amen

A Cry for Help

Out of the slavery their cry for help rose up to God.
                                                    —Exodus 2:23

My friend had a heart attack last night, and today, as the nurses wheeled him to surgery, he whispered to his wife, "I'm scared."

Those words were his cry for help. A man who is scared needs support, understanding, and encouragement. He's recovering from surgery, and now he needs not only medical skill; he has to stick to a low-fat diet, keep his spirits high, and start an exercise program.

That's where his friends come in. We can volunteer to accompany him on walks or go to the gym with him. When he comes to our houses for dinner, we'll serve the right foods. And when depression tries to overwhelm him, we'll be there to hold him up.

Maybe we who nibble, nibble, nibble need to say "I'm scared," and ask our friends and faith community for help. We might recover a lot faster.

FOR FURTHER REFLECTION

Can you admit to yourself you're scared? Scared of going without comfort foods; afraid to start one more exercise regimen that you might give up on; scared to admit you're powerless over food? Who is the best person for you to confide in?

PRAYER

Dear God, give me the courage to admit I'm scared. Amen

One Day at a Time

So do not worry about tomorrow, for tomorrow
will bring worries of its own.

—Matthew 6:34

The Twelve-Step slogan, "one day at a time," is about learning to live in the present. Yesterday is over and can't be changed; tomorrow is unpredictable. The only day I have is today, and the only person I can change is myself.

That sounds pretty limiting. But the worrywart who regrets the past, fears the future, and tries to control the world isn't liberated. Only people who live in present time and don't try to manage anyone but themselves are free.

The old song "Today" talks about not being able to live on promises. I can trust God's promises. What I need to forget is the stack of broken promises I've made to myself: *I'll lose thirty pounds; I'll never eat chocolate again; I'll stop with one helping.* "One day at a time" means forgetting those promises and deciding what I'm going to do right now.

FOR FURTHER REFLECTION

1. *Are you living one day at a time?*
2. *Can you give up regret about yesterday and fear about tomorrow?*
3. *How shall you live today?*

PRAYER

Loving Father, You created evenings and mornings so we could measure our lives. Help me to measure mine one day at a time.
Amen

Prisoner of Food

Bring me out of prison, so that I may give thanks
to your name.

—Psalm 142:7

If I were in jail, the bars would be made out of butter. I *love* butter, and I want it on my vegetables, my toast, and the rice cakes I like to eat at bedtime. Just the *thought* of a big mound of mashed potatoes with golden butter melting in the center makes my mouth water. And a plate of buttery cookies can completely destroy my self-discipline.

But if a jail's bars *were* made of butter, they'd melt. All the butter in the world, stacked in cubes higher than the Empire State Building, couldn't hold me in on a warm day.

I wonder how many times I've cowered inside the prison of food, feeling powerless, when God was trying to help me get free and find a new way of life. I'm going to start pushing through the "bars" today, and walk into freedom in the magnificent world around me.

FOR FURTHER REFLECTION

What are your prison's bars made of? Decide right now to break them down, or melt them, or plow through them, and be free.

PRAYER

You are the God who breaks every chain.
Set me free from the prison of food. Amen

Burying Anger

When King David heard of all these things, he became very angry,
but he would not punish his son . . . because he loved him . . .
—2 Samuel 13:21

Buried anger doesn't just dissolve. Unexpressed rage will always reappear as something like sarcasm, or depression, or compulsive shopping, or alcoholism. Or overeating.

Nothing whets my hunger like an unfinished argument, and there isn't a better appetizer than the wave of rage at what I perceive to be injustice. Trying to bottle up my anger makes me feel so impotent, the only thing I can do is head for the refrigerator.

I was past forty when I realized I didn't have to either blow up or bury my fury. I could *talk*. Not yell, not scold, not clam up; just talk. I finally learned to say what I thought without acting out my emotions, and I discovered that—when I had calmly said my piece—my anger had dissipated. And I hadn't wrecked anyone else's day.

FOR FURTHER REFLECTION

1. *How does burying your anger contribute to your overeating?*
2. *What can you do to change that?*

PRAYER

God of all joy and laughter, heal me of rage and hatred. Amen

Goal Addiction

*I press on toward the goal for the prize of
the heavenly call of God in Christ Jesus.*

—Philippians 3:14

Sometimes the goals I set for myself are absurdly high. But on the other hand, if I'm aiming for too *easy* a mark, I don't feel satisfied. Goals can be addictive: elusive, always promising happiness or riches or success.

The trick is making sure they're really my own objectives. When TV presents me with an actress who weighs ninety-two pounds, and whose wavy red hair falls to her waist, I don't have to try to be that person. When two of my friends go on crash diets to lose thirty pounds in three weeks, I can wish them well—but set my own target.

I need to listen for the goals God has in mind for me alone. Goals that will challenge me to be strong and brave and full of good humor. Perhaps what I most need to accomplish is making a rich strawberry trifle, piled high with whipped cream, for my guests—and not eating any of it myself. Your challenge may be quite different.

FOR FURTHER REFLECTION

1. *Are your goals too easy or too hard?*
2. *What sensible hard mark can you aim for today?*
3. *Do you beat yourself up when you miss the mark?*

PRAYER

Help me to strive, God, toward the goals You set for me. Amen

Wonderland

What do you know that we do not know?
What do you understand that is not clear to us?

—Job 15:9

When Alice fell through the rabbit hole into Wonderland, she found food that could make her tiny enough to get through a mouse hole or tall enough to look into birds' nests.

Late this afternoon I suddenly remembered that people were coming to dinner. I raced into the kitchen and as I stirred up a dessert for the dinner, a few spoonfuls of frosting seemed to say—like Alice's little cake—"Eat me!" As I prepared the appetizers, I succumbed to a handful of potato chips and a few dollops of sour cream. And while making the tamale pie, I managed to scarf down a handful of olives, some salsa, and several tablespoons of my beef-and-tomato mixture.

Maybe in Wonderland all those extra calories would only make me short or tall. But here on good old planet Earth, they head straight for my hips, thighs, and waist. Instead of being tall enough to look into birds' nests, I could get wide enough to require four or five airline seats.

So no matter where you are, it's a bad idea to let food talk you into eating. Chances are you know better than it does.

FOR FURTHER REFLECTION

1. *Are you listening to the "call" of food?*
2. *Do you pretend all those snacks won't count?*
3. *Are you ready to live on earth and face reality?*

PRAYER

Dear Lord, help me to be aware of the cumulative effect of all the "little" bits of food I grab without thinking in the course of a day.
Amen

Anesthetic for Pain

Jabez called on the God of Israel, saying,
"Oh that you would bless me . . . and keep me
from hurt and harm!"

—1 Chronicles 4:10

I was so upset I could hardly see. One of my best friends had turned on me during a meeting, and I wept all the way home. I stumbled into the house and groped my way to the refrigerator. But somewhere between grabbing the ice cream and getting the first spoon to my mouth, I realized what I was doing. I was eating to dull my pain.

Using ice cream or candy as an anesthetic has two unhappy results. First of all, of course, that kind of nibbling can make me fat and unhealthy. Second—and perhaps more serious—is the fact that if I don't face my pain immediately, that *pain* will grow fat and unhealthy and emerge later as a full-blown dragon that's harder to deal with.

Food won't kill my pain, but prayer can.

FOR FURTHER REFLECTION

On a journal page, jot down the things that make you turn to food: loneliness, frustration, pain, anger, boredom, depression. Underneath that list, write the number of problems food has actually solved for you.

PRAYER

Everlasting God, I look to food at times when I should turn to You. Forgive me, and help me see the truth of my life. Amen

Learning Hope

O my God, in you I trust; do not let me be put to shame;
do not let my enemies exult over me.

—Psalm 25:2

When Pandora opened her box, all the troubles in the world darted out. They attacked and stung her, and then flew through the door to trouble everyone else on earth. Afterward, one quiet little creature kept crying out from inside the box, and what weeping, wounded Pandora finally released was *hope*: God's gift to humanity.

It isn't always easy to keep a spirit of hope alive when magazines show me pictures of delicious food in living color, and every model on television looks like she weighs twelve pounds. But recently I saw a program that showed photographers gluing food together and enhancing its color with dyes and inks, and other camera people using a computer to shave inches off the waistline of the world's most famous model! Am I going to let photographers and computer artists deprive me of hope?

Hope has to be realistic. I can't hope God will appear like a wizard, waving a magic wand to make me thin and self-disciplined. But I *can* hope God will give me the wisdom to deal with overeating or any other aspect of my life.

FOR FURTHER REFLECTION

1. *What guides you most: hope or guilt?*
2. *What can you do when you begin to lose hope?*
3. *Are your hopes realistic?*

PRAYER

When I lose hope, Lord, I'm not keeping faith with You.
Catch me before I fall! Amen

The Mirror's Story

He made the basin of bronze with its stand of bronze,
from the mirrors of the women who served at the entrance
to the tent of meeting.

—Exodus 38:8

All Israel was busy creating the Tabernacle where God would reside. One of the items God commanded them to make was a bronze basin for ritual cleansing, where the priests would wash their hands before offering sacrifice or burning incense. Devout women gave up their highly polished bronze mirrors and let them be hammered into the basin. Those women traded vanity for purity.

I have a cousin who has for forty years lived in a Christian community with rules much like those of the Amish. The only mirror in her house is a small oval, just big enough for her and her husband to make sure their faces are clean. She was once a sophisticated world traveler who wore beautiful clothes and jewelry, but she traded her vanity (and *her* full-length mirror) for purity, too: a plain dress, a white apron, two simple meals a day, and a life without electricity or automobiles.

I don't have too strong an attachment to my mirror, but I would find life difficult without a computer or credit cards. And without those cupboards full of delicious snacks to nibble on. Can I trade those goodies for purity of conscience?

FOR FURTHER REFLECTION

1. *Do you spend too much time in front of the mirror, or thinking about yourself?*
2. *Do you need to abandon preoccupation with yourself?*
3. *For what quality could you trade this kind of vanity?*

PRAYER

Almighty God, turn my focus to You. Amen

Strength in Weakness

If I must boast, I will boast of the things
that show my weakness.
—2 Corinthians 11:30

As we raked the fallen autumn leaves under our hazelnut trees, squirrels and blue jays scrambled for the stray nuts. A big jay—one who had been announcing his presence in a raucous voice for some time—swooped down and picked up a choice nut, then flew up to sit on the fence, displaying his prize. He dropped it on the ledge and started to peck it open, but a small red squirrel, his tail waving like a flag, ran across the ledge and captured the nut.

The jay was furious, and began to quarrel with the squirrel, making pecking motions and screeching his displeasure. The squirrel dropped the hazelnut and fled, and the nut rolled to the ground, where a little sparrow, who had waited patiently, began to eat it. Humility had triumphed.

I don't have to scrounge for my food, or compete with other creatures for it. But I suspect I have a blue jay's self-centered heart and a squirrel's anxiety about food. Maybe I can learn to wait, like the sparrow.

FOR FURTHER REFLECTION

1. *What are some situations where you can practice more humility?*
2. *How does being humble differ from being humiliated?*
3. *How do you feel about practicing greater humility?*

PRAYER

Lord, You teach that humility is an attitude You want us to have.
Help me remember that. Amen

Life Should Be . . .

I call heaven and earth to witness against you today that I have set before you life and death, blessings and curses. Choose life . . .
—Deuteronomy 30:19

An old cartoon strip shows a couple talking as they emerge from a theater.

"The movies should be more like life," the woman says.

"No," her husband answers. "Life should be more like the movies."

Well, yes; wouldn't that be nice? In the movies and most television shows, houses stay clean by themselves, people already have enough money, and people eat whatever they want without gaining weight. If life were like the movies, we could do what we wanted without consequences, because characters in a movie only exist for two hours. They don't have to live forever with their choices.

But real people usually struggle through eighty years or more, facing new learning experiences every day. When Moses said, "Now choose life," he was talking about a daily decision. If I choose life for today, I'm choosing it also for tomorrow. If I say, "Today, I choose the life God gave me to live," I can't live recklessly for the rest of the week, stuffing my body full of candy and potato chips. Perhaps when I *really* choose life, I'll find satisfaction that lasts a lot longer than a chocolate bar.

FOR FURTHER REFLECTION

1. *Does your life reflect the kinds of choices you make?*
2. *Have you chosen real life, or just existence?*
3. *What do you choose today?*

PRAYER

Today I choose life, Lord, the life You offer in Scripture.
Please stay close to me. Amen

A Day on the Hill

The pastures of the wilderness overflow,
the hills gird themselves with joy.

—Psalm 65:12

My house is on a hillside in the last row of homes at the edge of the woods. I can take my camera up on the old logging road through the tall fir trees and bushy alders, or I can cut through the bushes to a now-abandoned quarry, where the rocky core of the hill is exposed.

Recently our relentless spring rain broke for a day. The sun came out and dazzled the flowers into bloom, clothed the trees with ripe green buds, and brought great clouds of birds to feed among the wild grasses. The hill was the scene of a party, and I spent most of the day in celebration. I stroked the pussy willows, breathed in the scent of freshened Douglas firs, and took close-up photographs of tiny yellow violets. I danced over the dark basalt rubble at the old quarry, and sang a hymn, sitting on a boulder under the trees.

That evening when I was getting ready for bed, I realized I hadn't nibbled *all day*. Beauty had satisfied all my senses, and I was filled not with food, but with the glory of God.

FOR FURTHER REFLECTION

What satisfies your senses and meets your emotional needs besides food? Take some time to find the answers, then act upon them.

PRAYER

Thank you, God, for the beauty of Your creation.
Teach me to be satisfied with that. Amen

Night Terrors

The Lord is your keeper; the Lord is your shade at your right hand.
The sun shall not strike you by day, nor the moon by night.

—Psalm 121:5, 6

I was a child who heard every sound in the night. Burglars and monsters lurked under the bed and in my padded window seat; but it was my closet that held the greatest terrors. I was sure I heard people in there, planning to burgle the house and perhaps take me away into the night.

My parents soothed me, turning on the light and showing me a closet full of nothing but clothes, a window seat holding nothing but toys and books. But the minute they left the darkened room, the ogres and kidnappers returned. One night when I called out in tears that someone was in my closet, my father brought in his deer rifle and blew a giant hole in the closet door.

"Got him that time," my father said. "He won't bother her any more." With that, he headed to his bed.

What he had actually shot was my new winter coat, and of course my mother was furious. But those monsters and burglars never came back. My father validated my feelings, and I was cured of my fear forever.

Now I need someone to blow a hole in my belief that I have to nibble all the time.

FOR FURTHER REFLECTION

When my father shot my closet door, he validated my feelings. Think back to a time when an adult made you feel affirmed. Where can you get that same affirmation today?

PRAYER

Eternal God, You are my protection and my reassurance.
Thank You. Amen

A Year-Long Day

*The beloved of the Lord rests in safety—the High God surrounds
him all day long—the beloved rests between his shoulders.*
—Deuteronomy 33:12

Since my grown daughter was having surgery early in the
morning, I tucked a breakfast bar in my purse and hurried to the
hospital. After she left for the operating room, I discovered a
nearby vending machine, so I bought some peanuts. After another
hour, I chose some corn chips and an apple.

After my daughter was in the recovery room, I went to the
hospital cafeteria for a bowl of soup and a sandwich. And so on.
The day was so long and so full of anxiety that I ate my way
through it; and after my daughter was in her own room and the
news was good, I celebrated with a candy bar. Some days, like that
one, feel as if they're a year long. Join fatigue to anxiety and
boredom, and you've laid the groundwork for an all-day nibbling
session.

Why didn't I pray instead of eating so much? Instead of
thumbing through old magazines in the waiting room, why didn't
I read my Bible? Now I'm trying to remember that God offers
refreshment all the time, and I don't have to drop coins in a
vending machine to get it.

FOR FURTHER REFLECTION

1. *Do you use stressful situations as occasions to nibble?*
2. *What could you do instead of eating?*
3. *How can you remind yourself to do that?*

PRAYER

*O God, grant me the wisdom to use my time for You
instead of food. Amen*

Who's at Work Here?

There are varieties of activities, but it is the same God who activates all of them in everyone.
—1 Corinthians 12:6

Sometimes I immediately notice that God has worked in my life. Once, for instance, when I was living unhappily in another state, someone called, offered me a job in the city where my kids lived (the employer didn't know that) and paid my transportation across country.

But other times, God lets me work for what I need. These devotions didn't just appear in my computer: I had to write, rewrite, edit, cut, and work hard to find every word.

So should I think God performed the miracle that got me home again, but just give myself the credit for writing or cooking or weeding? Hardly. When I re-read my devotions, I see God's fine hand at work. God gave me a love for cooking, and God's land produces the delicious fruits and vegetables I like to cook. And when all the weeds are pulled, I still can't take credit for the greenness of the grass. I suspect if I put in ten percent, God furnishes the other ninety.

So can you guess who's really working on my overeating?

FOR FURTHER REFLECTION

1. *Do you give God the credit for your life?*
2. *What percentage of your accomplishments can you take credit for?*
3. *Is God actively working on your nibbling?*

PRAYER

Thank You, God, for being the One who is always working in my life. Amen

Snapping

I am the Lord, who made all things . . .
who frustrates the omens of liars, and makes fools of diviners;
who turns back the wise, and makes their knowledge foolish.
—Isaiah 44:24, 25

In the sixth chapter of their book *Snapping*—based on their investigation of cults and why people join them—Flo Conway and Jim Siegelman write, "In all the world, there is nothing quite so impenetrable as a human mind snapped shut with bliss. No call to reason, no emotional appeal can get through its armor of self-proclaimed joy." Of course, what cult members perceive as "bliss" is the false euphoria produced by what we call "brainwashing." They've been told over and over that they will be free and happy when they adopt the rules of the cult.

Tonight my mind was snapped shut with phony bliss. The cause wasn't joining a cult or following some new false prophet; the cause was a quarter-pound chocolate bar. After the first nibble, my mind went into suspension and my taste buds began to run the show. The "cult" I joined was eating. Fortunately, nobody has to kidnap or deprogram me. In the nick of time—before I could think about eating anything else—God broke through, woke up my mind, and asked what I was doing. "Worshipping food again," I said.

FOR FURTHER REFLECTION

1. *Is your overeating a form of idolatry?*
2. *How can you deprogram yourself?*
3. *Are you praying daily for help with nibbling?*

PRAYER

Thank you, dear Lord, for the mind You gave me and the ability
to make good choices. Deliver me from the "cult"
of unnecessary food. Amen

Unprayed Prayer

*For what other great nation has a god so near to it
as the Lord our God is whenever we call to him?*

—Deuteronomy 4:7

Sometimes things happen so fast you just don't have time to pray. When you're dashing into the street to get your toddler out of the path of a car, or when you're slipping on ice, or when your pressure cooker is blowing up, you usually don't have the presence of mind to pray. At least not until the emergency is over. But I think God receives shock and terror as unprayed prayer.

Those unprayed prayers are free. The rest of the time, though, I'm supposed to pray—not for God's benefit, but for mine. When I pray, I become a better person. My faith is strengthened, I get out of myself for awhile, and I gain wisdom.

I don't think God considers *temptation* to be the kind of emergency where unprayed prayers count. When I'm staring through the bakery window at a tray of fresh éclairs, I have plenty of time to pray for help resisting. And when I sit down to dinner, not only can I thank God for the food, I can also ask for guidance in what and how much to eat.

FOR FURTHER REFLECTION

Make a list of some temptations you've had, and how prayer helped you overcome them. Then write out a prayer of thanksgiving for being delivered.

PRAYER

Thank You, Father, for all the times You've honored my fear or anxiety as prayer. Teach me by Your Holy Spirit how to pray at times of temptation. Amen

The Informed Heart

And this is my prayer, that your love may overflow more and more with knowledge and full insight.

—Philippians 1:9

I have a friend of many years who is the most affirming person I know. If I casually mention that I visited a sick friend, he responds by telling me what a wonderful work I'm doing for God. If my husband mentions his political views, my friend nods eagerly, and says that my husband is obedient: God is calling all Christians to exercise their political rights. He tells a crying child that it's wonderful to express the feelings God gives us. No matter what anyone does or says, he turns it into a victory for the Lord. He has an *informed* heart, one that not only loves, but also understands. A heart that knows all the facts, and still acts with affirmation.

Knowing I'm a sinner, knowing I'm sometimes guilty of sloth or envy or overeating, God still affirms me and treats me with compassion and kindness. My overeating doesn't endanger my salvation; God just thinks it's not good for me. And I agree.

FOR FURTHER REFLECTION

1. *Is your heart informed so that you can build up the body of Christ?*
2. *Are you grateful for God's informed heart?*
3. *How does thinking about this affect your nibbling?*

PRAYER

Lord, Your heart is totally informed, and You treat Your children with unconditional love. Inform my heart so that I am a help to myself and others. Amen

Making Food Work for Me

And the Lord God commanded the man,
"You may freely eat of every tree of the garden . . ."
—Genesis 2:16

In the beginning, God gave human beings a perfect diet that would make their bodies work properly and also taste good. If taste hadn't been a factor, God could have appointed only one plant or fruit to nourish our bodies. But God made us capable of enjoyment, and created taste buds and the sense of pleasure.

Our lives reveal that we have fallen. We were made for action, yet too many of us are couch potatoes. And we were created to eat food that would taste good and be enjoyable, but a majority of Americans are either overweight or have eating disorders such as anorexia or bulimia.

The answer has to be in Jesus, who redeemed us through his death and resurrection. We are no longer prisoners of fallenness, but we can be released from bondage to overeating by the blood of Jesus. And we can learn to let food work the way God intended.

And that's the thought I want to hold onto the next time I think I need a candy bar.

FOR FURTHER REFLECTION

1. *Can you admit your own, personal fallenness and need for Jesus?*
2. *Is your overeating a sign of this condition?*
3. *How can you redeem your time on earth?*

PRAYER

I lack only one thing, Lord: a grateful heart.
Help me remember the price You paid for me. Amen

Dear Intruder

Very truly, I tell you, anyone who does not enter the sheepfold by
the gate but climbs in by another way is a thief and a bandit.
The one who enters by the gate is the shepherd of the sheep.
—John 10:1, 2

Jesus never lets me alone for long. He's an intruder, a dear intruder, always present, waiting for my attention and response. He doesn't force His opinions on me, but He does express them often. The minute I begin to wander from Christian life and work, I hear His words from the Bible, dancing through my head.

It's my own doing. I invited Jesus into my heart and I'm sure you know that if you give Him an inch, He'll take a mile. You ask for enough strength to do a little work, and He gives you plenty—along with a hundred new jobs. Pray for patience, and God will keep giving you situations where you learn it. And beg for a little help to stop nibbling so much, and you don't just stop snacking: the next thing you know, you're taking vitamins and exercising.

However, now that I've expressed my momentary discomfort with Jesus' remodeling job in my life, I have to admit that I'm starting to feel pretty good.

FOR FURTHER REFLECTION

1. *How is Jesus changing your life?*
2. *Do you appreciate these changes, or are you dragging your feet?*

PRAYER

Welcome, dear Intruder; I offer You my life as a home. Amen

Closer Than Breath

Let everything that breathes praise the Lord! Praise the Lord!
—Psalm 150:6

My friend Linda sometimes had trouble knowing God as more than a Punisher. In Linda's mind, dietary restrictions were punishments. "I know it's wrong," she said recently, "but trying to lose weight feels as if God has sent me to the corner for being naughty."

Over the next few weeks, Linda ordered salads when everyone else was having ice cream. At first she grumbled about not being able to eat what she wanted, when she wanted. But gradually she began to change her mind about the new way she was eating. She stopped seeing a Punisher who wanted to starve her into submission. She started believing God longed to help her with the effort to quit nibbling.

When Linda accepted that God wasn't mad at her for overeating, it was easier to learn to eat healthy foods. I, too, want to remember that God is always closer than breath and always willing to help.

FOR FURTHER REFLECTION

1. *Do you think God is punishing you for being overweight?*
2. *Are you afraid God will give up on you?*
3. *Will you allow yourself to feel that God is close to you?*

PRAYER

Dear God, I need to feel Your presence today. Amen

Pork Chop Before Dawn

Stolen water is sweet, and bread eaten in secret is pleasant.
—Proverbs 9:17

The open fridge cast an eerie light in the kitchen where I stood, eating leftover pork chops. I'd tiptoed down the hall so no one else would know I had gone straight for the plate of chops. Gnawing on a bone, I saw my own reflection in the window. My first thought was that I'd caught myself raiding the kitchen. My second was how good the chops tasted when I believed no one was looking.

Some bank robbers steal for the thrill. I often feel the same rush if I sneak a morsel when no one's around. I may refuse seconds at the family table and order rabbit food in restaurants, but I'm not helping myself if I eat in secret. I know come morning I'll feel as guilty as if I'd robbed a bank, not stolen a pork chop. Stolen food may taste delicious but it gives me heartburn. I think God wants me to remember to be more open and honest about my eating habits.

FOR FURTHER REFLECTION

Today, be your own detective. Keep track of how much you eat when you are alone, compared to when you are dining with family or friends. Then ask God for help if you tend to be a lonesome nibbler. You may be eating in private because you are ashamed to eat in public.

PRAYER

Lord, please take away the shame I feel when I eat. Amen

Saying Yes to Change

I am about to do a new thing; now it springs forth,
do you not perceive it?

—Isaiah 43:19

A Spanish proverb says, "Mañana is the busiest day of the week." When it comes to nibbling, I admit I often resolve to cut back on snacks tomorrow, after I've already blown it for today. As long as the plan starts tomorrow I can shave off another sliver of leftover birthday cake or filch a few extra cashews. It's afterwards that I quickly adopt a get tough attitude, commanding myself to change mañana.

But by noon the next day my resolve dissolves. I finish off the kids' oatmeal, lick the peanut butter knife when I make their lunches, and pour cream instead of skim milk into my coffee. I feel defeated because I nibbled, so I begin to rationalize: Today's a total loss. I'll try again, tomorrow.

Falling into the trap of procrastination is easy. And climbing out is hard—unless God lends me a hand. As I reach to God, I want to remember that my overeating can stop any time I want—whether or not I've already blown it for today. Each time I refuse to nibble, I'm getting a jumpstart on tomorrow.

FOR FURTHER REFLECTION

1. *If you nibble today do you really have to wait until tomorrow to start over?*
2. *Are you ready for a change?*
3. *Will you let God help you start today?*

PRAYER

God, help me say yes to change. Amen

Porpoises

Rejoice in that day and leap for joy,
for surely your reward is great in heaven.

—Luke 6:23

Porpoises and dolphins at places like Sea World leap and pirouette on command, dazzling audiences. Children and adults flock to watch these intelligent mammals put on a show. But in the wild, porpoises and dolphins also leap and spin as part of their natural behavior. No one commands them to perform on the open seas. Do they leap for the sheer joy of being alive?

Often I think I need a good reason to be happy, and just as often I think I can't possibly be happy until I lose a few pounds. I tell myself that when I finally get control of my weight, I'll be able to see the joy in life again; as soon as I learn to say no to bad eating habits, my life will overflow with happiness.

Yet God doesn't want me to live in the future. He wants me to be joyful *now*. No matter how slow my progress, I can still feel good about trying to change. Like a porpoise, I don't need a special reason to rejoice. I can leap for joy every day—even before I have my nibbling totally under control.

FOR FURTHER REFLECTION

1. *Are there things in your life you can be joyful about?*
2. *Does nibbling make your sorrows disappear?*
3. *If you're leaping for joy, will you still want to nibble?*

PRAYER

Dear God, open my eyes to joy today. Amen

Twenty Questions

Solomon answered all her questions; there was nothing hidden from the king that he could not explain to her.

—1 Kings 10:3

In a way, nibbling is like riding a bicycle: I never forget how. Put a plate of warm, fresh-baked cookies in front of me and I take the bait without thinking. Leave a bowl of chips around and I'll feel sorry for them, eating them so they won't go to waste.

I often nibble without thinking. Then I feel defeated. But what if I stop first and ask myself a few questions? Playing the twenty questions game with myself might help me to understand why I want to nibble. Am I really hungry? Do I lack animal, vegetable, or mineral nutrients? Am I just reaching for a handful of something because I'm or worried or bored?

I'll ask God. If I listen closely, I'll hear the answers to my questions as I go before the King. If I slow down, I may decide I'm not hungry right now after all. Maybe I'll go ride that bike instead of eating.

FOR FURTHER REFLECTION

When you feel like nibbling, stop and ask yourself if you're really hungry. Wait ten minutes. If you're still hungry, eat a small portion of something healthy, such as fruit or raw vegetables.

PRAYER

Heavenly Father, help me remember to eat only when I'm hungry.
Amen

Elephant in the . . . Kitchen?

O God, you know my folly; the wrongs I have done
are not hidden from you.

—Psalm 69:5

An important children's book, *An Elephant in the Living Room*, deals with alcoholism and addiction in families. Nobody will mention the huge behemoth that has knocked over lamps and is probably crushing the couch; the entire family pretends the elephant isn't there, even though it is ruining their lives.

In our house, the elephant is in the kitchen. I don't talk about being addicted to nibbling, and neither does my husband, who is diabetic and has a serious weight problem. Once in awhile, one of us will whisper the word "elephant," but we quickly change the subject. Just like the family in the children's book, we're pretending the elephant isn't there.

Unlike drinking and drugs, my nibbling can't ruin someone else's life, but it can ruin *mine*. I've got to admit to others that there's a big beast in my kitchen.

FOR FURTHER REFLECTION

1. *Do you have an elephant in your kitchen or pantry?*
2. *Have you pretended it wasn't there?*
3. *Are you willing to admit to another person that you're addicted to nibbling?*

PRAYER

Lord, help me extricate the elephant from my life;
teach me to face the truth. Amen

Water Stories

Then God opened her eyes and she saw a well of water.
—Genesis 21:19

The Bible is filled with water stories. An angel showed Hagar a well, so her child did not die of thirst. Rebekah watered Abraham's servant's camels at a well, and was betrothed as a result. Jacob met his future wife at what was probably the same well. And so on. At the end of the Bible we read, "Come. And let everyone who is thirsty come. Let anyone who wishes take the water of life as a gift."

In desert country, water and wells are of vital importance. Abraham and Isaac both had disputes with nomadic tribes over water rights. Even today, some of the disputes between Israel and Palestine have to do with water rights, so water is still a precious commodity.

All I have to do to get water is turn on a faucet or take a plastic bottle out of my purse. But as easy as it is for me to find this most vital resource, I don't seem to fully appreciate how truly valuable it is. Water is there for me to quench my thirst, to keep my body functioning properly, and to fill me up when I might otherwise grab something fattening instead. Why aren't I drinking it all the time?

FOR FURTHER REFLECTION

1. *Do you give water much thought?*
2. *How much water do you drink a day?*
3. *Do you appreciate how helpful water can be in controlling your appetite?*

PRAYER

O Lord, help me to see the wells of precious water
You have supplied to quench my thirst. Amen

Cool Hand Luke

And though you eat, you shall not be satisfied.
—Leviticus 26:26

In the movie *Cool Hand Luke*, the protagonist—an inmate in a corrupt prison system—says he can eat fifty hard-boiled eggs. His fellow prisoners take bets and make big preparations in a party-like atmosphere, and Luke becomes a kind of hero to them. Luke wouldn't be eating for satisfaction, but to prove a point and win a bet.

I like to joke that if they were *deviled* eggs, I might be able to eat fifty. But stuff myself with that much food at one time? And all one kind of food?

Actually, that thought leads me to realize I probably sometimes ingest the caloric equivalent of what Cool Hand Luke did. I know that at one sitting, I can consume a whole bag of potato chips or an entire box of See's chocolates, I guess because I like the taste. I need to learn how to set limits—how to stop eating when my hunger has abated. Eating slowly and thoughtfully and prayerfully may be a way to start.

FOR FURTHER REFLECTION

1. *Are you addicted to flavor?*
2. *Do you let taste rule your life?*
3. *How quickly do you eat?*
4. *Do you know when to say "enough"?*

PRAYER

Dear God, You have provided me with enough food to keep me alive and satisfied. Now I ask for one more thing: temperance in eating. Amen

Politics

So the presidents and the satraps tried to find grounds for complaint against Daniel in connection with the kingdom. But they could find no grounds for complaint or any corruption, because he was faithful, and no negligence or corruption could be found in him.

—Daniel 6:4

Even people who rarely pay attention to politics were riveted to news channels after the 2000 presidential election. November became December and we still weren't sure who would be President of the United States. Then the Supreme Court made its ruling, and the "long count" was all over.

So were the excitement and suspense. And because I'm a news junkie who loves anything political, I suddenly felt let down. My work was a little ragged for a day or two, and I found myself in the kitchen, spreading peanut butter on crackers, sipping eggnog, munching holiday cookies and rich fruit cake. One day I realized I was eating my third chocolate pecan candy—and it was only ten-thirty in the morning.

Thank goodness for my journal. I curled up in the living room and began to write down all my feelings about the election: my joys, disappointments, fears, delights, and my attitude about the final outcome. I wrote about eight pages, and when I was through, I had writer's cramp; but I didn't feel restless—or hungry—any more.

FOR FURTHER REFLECTION

1. *Are you really in touch with your feelings?*
2. *Are you turning to food to make up for something else?*
3. *Would writing in a journal help you quit nibbling?*

PRAYER

Almighty God, remind me that feelings and emotions are powerful. Help me recognize them. Amen

Goldfinches

By the streams the birds of the air have their habitation;
they sing among the branches.

—Psalm 104:12

The goldfinches usually arrive in late May, surging through our city in small flocks, turning trees into yellow clouds, and crowding backyard bird feeders. I am constantly amazed at how much they eat, and I've read that a goldfinch usually consumes more than its own weight every day.

Whoa! I couldn't swallow or digest more than a hundred pounds a day, much less metabolize it. But fast-flying little birds like goldfinches use up an incredible amount of energy. They make up to ten thousand trips for nesting material, and about a thousand forays for food each day. That doesn't count the unexplained festivals that birds have, when they dart into the sky in great flocks, soaring, turning, wheeling through the sky. Goldfinch eggs incubate in about twelve days, and in twelve more, the birdlings fledge!

But I sit most of the day in front of a computer, not moving anything except my eyes and my fingers. So I guess I better not try to eat like a bird.

FOR FURTHER REFLECTION

God doesn't expect you to expend as much energy as a bird; but try writing two lists: one of the number of calories you eat in a day, and another of how much exercise you get to burn them up. What will you discover?

PRAYER

You designed the birds and the beasts to eat what they need, God. Help me do the same thing. Amen

Sore Feet, Warm Heart

For I was hungry and you gave me food,
I was thirsty and you gave me something to drink,
I was a stranger and you welcomed me.
—Matthew 25:35

Our church participates in a winter program to feed and shelter homeless families. For a week, thirty people live in the fellowship hall of our church, sleeping on the mattresses provided by a local religious charity; each family has privacy screens provided by the same charity.

One of my duties during this week is to serve food and entertain the children. The kids aren't always a happy, easy group: they're angry about their situation, and they don't really know each other well enough to be thrown together so much. So I serve them and their parents the dinner our volunteers have prepared from donated food, and then I tell stories, lead games, and present some kind of craft.

When I got home last night, after a long valentine-making session where I stood, walked, helped cut and paste, and handed out candy, I got home with sore feet but a warm heart. And guess what? I hadn't nibbled a bite of dessert or candy. Love satisfied me.

FOR FURTHER REFLECTION

1. *Are you feeding the hungry, helping the homeless, or doing other charitable works?*
2. *How do you feel when you're busy helping others?*
3. *Do you need to change anything about your spare time and money?*

PRAYER

Dear God, fill my heart with love and charity.
Show me how to care for others. Amen

Doubt

But ask in faith, never doubting, for the one who doubts
is like a wave of the sea, driven and tossed by the wind;
for the doubter, being double-minded and unstable in every way,
must not expect to receive anything from the Lord.

—James 1:6, 7

Shakespeare said our doubts were traitors that made us lose the good we might have won because we were afraid to try. When I look back on my life, at the many times I've tried to stop overeating, I see the shadow of doubt's wings over those attempts. I don't doubt the premise of eating healthier food, and I don't doubt that I *could* do it if I believed in myself. What I doubt is me.

Deep down, where nobody else can see, is a scared kid who's afraid of failure. If I don't try, I can't fail, can I? Although my intellect tells me not to doubt myself, my emotions are still running at that scared-kid level. So first I need to bring that frightened little girl into the present, where she can see that success is possible.

How do I do this? Prayerfully. Because no matter how much I doubt myself, I don't doubt God, or God's ability to get me on the right track.

FOR FURTHER REFLECTION

Look into your heart, and see if there's a frightened person inside you, one who is afraid to try. Every day for a week, write yourself a letter, convincing yourself to come out into the sunshine and make a new attempt at eating healthfully. End each letter with the words "And God will help you."

PRAYER

I'm having doubts, Lord, and they are setting me up for failure.
Please help me learn to believe in myself and in
Your unfailing help. Amen

Great and Marvelous

I do not occupy myself with things
too great and too marvelous for me.

—Psalm 131:1

My friend watched with something like awe as I scanned into my computer the battered old picture of her grandmother as a young girl. I opened it in my graphics program, arranged a frame design around it, made it into a greeting card, and printed it on heavy photo paper. She had a special birthday greeting for her grandmother.

"I watched everything you did, but I could never repeat it," she wailed. "You grasp something I don't understand at all."

However, the next time we were together, she helped me balance my checkbook and complete my income tax return. Now it was my turn to be awed. I hate arithmetic and I have as little to do with numbers as possible; her adding and allocating were amazing.

Clearly, my friend and I have very different gifts. We also have very different personalities. She's outgoing and full of feeling, and I'm more introverted and serious. But we share one thing: we both nibble. And together, we're a powerhouse! So now we're trying to use our separate gifts to support each other in the fight against overeating.

FOR FURTHER REFLECTION

1. *How do you use your gifts to serve others?*
2. *Do you turn to friends for support and inspiration?*
3. *How hard is it to admit your nibbling problem to others?*

PRAYER

I need support, God. Show me where I can find a friend
or a group. Amen

Stiff-necked Pride

They have stiffened their necks, refusing to hear my words.
—Jeremiah 19:15

My friend Sarah was a size two for most of our adult lives. All through her twenties, this gorgeous and intelligent woman ate gobs of french fries, but never gained an ounce. Even the birth of two children didn't alter Sarah's svelte figure. Fast food was her constant companion—until she hit her thirties. Then the pounds began to creep on.

Sarah wouldn't acknowledge that fast food might be responsible. One day she took a long hard look in the mirror and realized pride was her real enemy. As long as she refused to let God help her get control of her nibbling, she knew she'd never change.

She began to seek God's help with her eating habits and slowly her jeans got looser. Today, I want to put aside my own pride and let God help me, too, even when I hear, "Do you want fries with that?"

FOR FURTHER REFLECTION

1. *Are there certain foods you don't want to give up?*
2. *Is pride keeping you from changing?*
3. *Are you willing to let God help you with your nibbling?*

PRAYER

Dear Lord, help me put my pride aside today. Amen

The Vineyard

I am the vine, you are the branches.
Those who abide in me and I in them bear much fruit,
because apart from me you can do nothing.

—John 15:5

Grapes appear only on new growth, so every fall vineyard workers cut grapevines back to the classic bare "T" shape. The next year's grape-bearing branches are already contained in the vine's DNA and growth patterns. The promise of grapes is *abiding*, over the winter, in the bare brown stem.

In the spring, the vine sends out scores of thick green branches, at first leafy but eventually heavy with clusters of dark purple golden grapes. Commercial vineyard workers hover over the vines like mother birds, bracing a branch here, cutting off a fruitless one there. No sprouts or suckers are allowed to flourish on their own; only the branches that have abided in the main trunk are able to bear fruit.

I certainly don't want to be cut off and thrown into the fire. So if I want to be a holy branch, I need to think about how my overeating is affecting my spiritual life. And vice versa.

FOR FURTHER REFLECTION

1. How do you think a person "abides" in Christ?
2. Are you content to be a branch, or do you want to be the whole vine?
3. How is your nibbling affecting your prayer life?

PRAYER

Make me a fruitful branch, dear Lord. Amen

Know-It-All

The proud, haughty person, named "Scoffer,"
acts with arrogant pride.

—Proverbs 21:24

Have you ever told someone you were cutting calories, only to hear, "I've got the perfect diet for you"? If you resolve to change your eating habits, suddenly you get inundated with advice. Diet programs claim they'll slim your waist in record time. Even your spouse and your best friend think they know just what you need.

I've given my share of unsolicited eating advice and I've tried all manner of weight-loss methods. I've been on grapefruit diets, protein shakes, no-carbohydrate and all-carbohydrate plans. I've tried to quit nibbling by drinking so much water I thought I'd float away. Most of these fads came and went with little success. I've found the one surefire way to manage my nibbling has been to take advice only from my doctor and from God.

The next time someone tells me they are trying to work on their eating, I think I'll forgo giving advice and offer to pray instead. I know how hard it can be to become an ex-nibbler. It makes more sense to dish out a little support.

FOR FURTHER REFLECTION

1. *Are you ready to give up food fads?*
2. *Do you need to tell your doctor about these habits?*
3. *Can you seek God's advice about nibbling?*

PRAYER

God, I want to hear only Your advice today. Amen

To Walk and Not Faint

But those who wait for the Lord shall renew their strength,
they shall mount up with wings like eagles,
they shall run and not be weary, they shall walk and not faint.
                                                    —Isaiah 40:31

On days when food gets the best of me, the only exercise I undertake is lifting my hand to my mouth. Especially during the winter, when it's cold or snowy or raining, the last thing I want to do is move around. The temptation to park myself somewhere with a good book and a bag of something delicious is almost too hard to resist. Then I remember how good I feel after a brisk walk.

In bad weather I walk in a nearby shopping mall, before the shops open. The rest of the time I try to walk outdoors every day, even if it's only to the mailbox. The German philosopher Frederick Nietzsche once said that every truly great thought is conceived while walking. I'm not sure I think great thoughts when I walk, but I do notice some other benefits. Walking gets my heart rate up, decreases my appetite and gives me time to pray. Nibbling the day away becomes less important when I'm busy exercising my heart, my mind, and my spirit.

FOR FURTHER REFLECTION

Ask a friend or loved one to join you for a walk today. If you can't find a partner, talk to God while you walk.

PRAYER

Lord, help me to get moving today. Amen

Spelling Bee

Let the young men come forward
and have a contest before us.

—2 Samuel 2:14

In seventh grade I won the school spelling bee and advanced to the district contest. But being a champion speller wasn't much fun for me. Every year I'd get sick and withdraw before the competition began. I knew in my heart that I got sick because I was afraid to lose. If I couldn't be perfect I wouldn't try at all.

I sometimes take the same approach to controlling my eating. If I can't live on two soy beans and a lettuce leaf, I stop trying. Soon food has an even stronger hold on me and I'm stuck in an endless contest.

I think God wants me to know that I can win the nibbling game, but I don't have to be perfect. God will help me if I fall. I don't have to lose anything but fear and, if I keep at it, a few inches around my waist. That's how I spell success.

FOR FURTHER REFLECTION

1. *Do you consider weight management a contest?*
2. *Do you give up first, so you don't have to face failure?*
3. *Are you willing just to do your best?*

PRAYER

Heavenly Father, help me keep going even if I'm not perfect. Amen

Child of the Light

*And the city has no need of sun or moon to shine on it,
for the glory of God is its light, and its lamp is the Lamb.*
—Revelation 21:23

Kathleen Thomerson's hymn, "I Want to Walk as a Child of the Light" echoes John's words in Revelation that the Lamb—that is, Jesus—is the lamp of the City of God. John wasn't talking about something plugged into an electric outlet. A lamp was a container of oil with a wick on one end.

I own such an ancient lamp: a small red clay king, lying on his back, with a large hole in his chest for pouring oil, and a smaller aperture at his feet, for the wick. The figure reclines in a vulnerable position: with his chest open and his feet aflame, he can hardly rise up to take arms or wave his scepter. He is powerless—yet without him, his original owner would have had no light.

I have spiritual light only because Christ made Himself powerless on the cross. He sheds His light on me, and I want to walk as a child of that light. Now how does that change my eating?

FOR FURTHER REFLECTION

1. *Is Jesus Christ the lamp of your life?*
2. *Do you let that light shine on your nibbling?*
3. *Does seeing your eating through that light make you feel more in control?*

PRAYER

You are the light of my life, God. Amen

The Jug of Oil

The jar of meal was not emptied, neither did the jug of oil fail,
according to the word of the Lord that he spoke by Elijah.
—1 Kings 17:16

Elijah lived with a poor widow and her son during a three-year famine. Though they had no money to buy food, they never ran out of oil and flour for their daily bread.

When I shop for groceries, I sometimes act as if I'm afraid I might run out of food. My cupboards and freezer are packed, my breadbox is packed, and I discovered recently that I had six different jars of honey that I'd bought "just in case."

In case of what? Fire? Flood? Famine? I don't have to worry about the Y2K bug any longer, or the volcano more than a hundred miles north of us. My husband is diabetic and doesn't eat honey, so about the only time I use it is to make an occasional loaf of bread.

What am I stocking up for? I wonder if deep down in me, I'm afraid I'll wander to the kitchen at midnight—and find nothing to snack on. What I have to do now is face that panic and live without nibbling.

FOR FURTHER REFLECTION

Take an inventory of your food supply. Do the contents of your cupboards tell you anything about your state of mind or your relationship with food?

PRAYER

Loving Father, teach me to trust that You will never
leave me wanting. Amen

Zebra Stripes

He shall be a wild ass of a man,
with his hand against everyone,
and everyone's hand against him;
and he shall live at odds with all his kin.

—Genesis 16:12

How can a zebra be so much like a horse, yet so unlike it in temperament? You can saddle a horse, and ride it; you can hitch it to a wagon, or ask it to leap over fences and hedges. When I was a child, I was lucky enough to have my own horse to ride, and I loved her like a good friend.

But most zebras usually can't or won't be tamed. Although Grevy's zebra is the closest living relative of the horse ancestor from which all modern horses, donkeys, and zebras were born, you don't see bareback riders standing on the backs of zebras, or cowboys riding the striped creatures to round up the cattle. Zebras are testy, and quick to bite or kick when anyone annoys them.

Sometimes I act as if I have zebra blood. Every time God leads me toward better eating habits, I begin to bite and kick and run away. I think it's time I get the bit in my mouth instead of so much fattening food.

FOR FURTHER REFLECTION

Today, decide whether you want to be a horse, living in harmony with God, or a wild zebra, independent and hostile to God's leading.

PRAYER

Take away my zebra stripes, Lord, and teach me obedience. Amen

Parades

Each keeps to its own course,
they do not swerve from their paths.

—Joel 2:7

In Ireland, a parade is a powerful political event. "Orange" parades through Catholic villages are considered tantamount to acts of war, but in America we have trouble imagining such grief and anger. The kinds of parades we're used to, with floats, marching bands, baton twirlers, and ornamented horses, are a particularly American production. Free circus street marches evolved in the United States and a parade was part of the first Independence Day celebration. Parades have become more elaborate every year, with floats made of flowers and with thousands of fresh-faced youth drumming and piping before New Years' bowl games, during Mardi Gras, at presidential inaugurations, and to advertise Christmas shopping.

On days when I control my nibbling, I feel like having a parade down our street, with an elephant or two, a band playing "Hail the Conquering Hero Comes," and a banner that proclaims my victory. If I stay the course I'd like the whole world to celebrate with me.

FOR FURTHER REFLECTION

Today, start a victory journal. Every time you manage to avoid nibbling, write down the date and give yourself a gold star or another symbol to recognize your achievement. Include your comments on what strengthened your resolve and how you overcame temptation.

PRAYER

I celebrate Your presence in my life, God.
Show me how to be victorious yet humble. Amen

Bird Food

He gives snow like wool; he scatters frost like ashes.
He hurls down hail like crumbs—who can stand before his cold?
—Psalm 147:16, 17

We had such a hard freeze the fallen leaves stuck to the ground, and birds seeking food couldn't scratch in the earth. My daughter and I watched the desperate birds, trying to find food, and wanted to help. I didn't dare drive to the store—cars were sliding into one another everywhere—and it was too far even to try walking.

So we started chopping up breads and cakes: a stollen, cupcakes, some Finnish rye. We distributed the crumbs all over my deck railing, and filled my bird feeders. The chickadees came first, eagerly feasting, and after them, the big starlings swooped down to eat. Juncos and piñon jays joined the party, so we crumbled a box of graham crackers and chopped some frozen tortillas.

Those birds weren't greedy; they were starving.

Then on Sunday, I went to church and took Communion. Bread had a whole new meaning; I was starving in a different way, and God fed me.

FOR FURTHER REFLECTION

Today, hang a bird feeder outside your window; if you can't do that, buy some bird seed and scatter it in your yard or a city park. Also buy yourself a bottle of grape juice and a small loaf of bread. While the birds enjoy your generosity, enjoy God's.

PRAYER

Thank You for the birds, Lord,
and for all of Your gifts to me. Amen

Love Unknown

From this time forward I make you hear new things,
hidden things that you have not known.

—Isaiah 48:6

My favorite hymn is "My Song Is Love Unknown," written in the 1700s by Samuel Crossman. The first verse says, "My song is love unknown, my Savior's love to me; Love to the loveless shown, That they might lovely be." That hymn reminds me that God is always at work around me, trying to break through my presupposed notions in order to show me a kind of love about which I still know nothing.

The line "that they might lovely be" doesn't mean God is trying to make me thinner or younger or prettier. "Lovely" in the eighteenth century meant loving, full of the kind of mercy and tenderness God wants us to have.

I probably spend more time thinking about being "lovely" in the modern sense of the word—having to do with outward appearance—than about being "lovely" by Crossman's standards. So maybe I should concentrate more on, say, feeding the homeless than on overfeeding myself.

FOR FURTHER REFLECTION

1. *Are you so focused on your own shortcomings that you miss opportunities to show love?*
2. *Is God trying to make you "lovelier"?*

PRAYER

He came from His blest throne
Salvation to bestow;
But men made strange, and none
The longed for Christ would know:
But O! my Friend, my Friend indeed,
Who at my need His life did spend.

—Samuel Crossman

Reveille

I lie down and sleep;
I wake again, for the Lord sustains me.

—Psalm 3:5

Our camp counselors used a gong so raucous I would almost jump out of my sleeping bag at reveille. But after that morning gong I always fell back to sleep. I was ten years old and had trouble sleeping away from home, so most nights I read *A Tale of Two Cities* under the covers with a flashlight until almost dawn. I usually didn't join the group until sometime after breakfast. By the afternoon, I was having a good time swimming and riding, and by nightfall I'd be singing around the camp fire.

Until the day when reveille didn't wake me at all from a deep, feverish sleep. Nobody missed me at breakfast, but at noon a counselor found me comatose. I had mosquito-borne encephalitis. Sleeping sickness. Even Gabriel's trumpet wouldn't have aroused me.

I'd been in a coma for three weeks when a hospital worker dropped a bedpan and it crashed to the floor. I sat upright, looked at my mother, who'd been keeping vigil in the chair by my bed, and said, "Reveille. I've got to get up."

Gonnnggg! If God were sending me a loud wake-up call today about my eating habits would I hear it?

FOR FURTHER REFLECTION

1. *Do you have a tendency to hit the snooze button when your morning alarm goes off?*
2. *Are you putting healthier eating habits on snooze instead of heeding the alarm?*
3. *Is it time for you to respond to reveille?*

PRAYER

Dear God, help me to hear You calling me
to a healthier way of life. Amen

It's More Than Possible

All things can be done
for the one who believes.

—Mark 9:23

Remember the little blue engine that chugged "I think I can, I think I can"? I think some days, my little engine says, "I thought I could, but I couldn't." I sometimes get discouraged and decide that trying to get my eating habits under control is useless.

But God keeps nudging me, the way a mother horse keeps nudging and licking her newborn foal until he's standing on his feet. I hear God's voice whispering, "Yes, you can. Keep trying." So maybe I can.

Why does God care whether I quit nibbling? God knows I care, and what matters to me matters to God. When I overeat, I feel guilty and out of order. I don't have that triumphant sense of self-discipline that makes me feel fit for God's company.

I can't do it alone. I know that now. But with God's strength and His constant nudging and encouragement, I can do it.

FOR FURTHER REFLECTION

1. *What can you do to push away discouragement?*
2. *Would it help you to write down your negative feelings?*
3. *Are you turning to God every day for encouragement?*

PRAYER

Yes, Lord, with Your help I can and I will. Amen

Precious in God's Sight

When you pass through the waters, I will be with you;
and through the rivers, they shall not overwhelm you;
when you walk through fire you shall not be burned,
and the flame shall not consume you. . . .
you are precious in my sight, and honored, and I love you.
—Isaiah 43:2, 4

The wind woke me up, dashing rain against the outside wall of my bedroom. In my nightshirt, I raced outside and began pulling plastic over half-ripe tomatoes, crunchy leaf lettuce, and pods full of snap peas. As I knelt to cover the baby beets, I got soaked, and pelted by fierce hail, but I saved the precious food in my garden.

I went inside to put on dry clothes and wrap my hair in a towel, thinking that when you grow food, you recognize its value. In fact, anything you fight for becomes important, so after fighting the world for me all my life, God must see me as precious. Whether I'm passing through the waters or walking through fire, or just struggling with my nibbling, God is on my side, taking as much care of me as I do my tender young vegetables.

FOR FURTHER REFLECTION

1. *Do you recognize how precious you are in God's sight?*
2. *Do you treat yourself with the same care you give your garden?*
3. *What can you do to take better care of yourself?*

PRAYER

Thank you, Lord, for covering and protecting me
in the storm of life. Help me to honor Your investment in me.
Amen

Run with Patience

Therefore, since we are surrounded by so great a cloud of witnesses,
let us also lay aside every weight and the sin that clings so closely,
and let us run with perseverance the race that is set before us.
—Hebrews 12:1

My friend Lilly had become severely asthmatic; she could walk only a few steps before she started to wheeze. She was spending most of her days in front of the window, looking out at a world she'd had to give up. One day she watched a crowd of people in green tank tops and shorts, running down the street and sidewalks in one of our many Oregon 10K races. She turned to her husband and said, "I want to run."

He laughed. So did her doctor. But Lilly began building herself up, taking her medicine and praying. She walked the length of the block, then around the block and beyond. Finally, she began to run, at first a half-mile, then a mile. . . . Her doctor reduced her prescriptions because her lungs were working better. Three years after that day when she sat at the window, Lilly ran the entire ten-kilometer race.

"I didn't get the trophy," she said, "but I won." Lilly had run her race with perseverance—and with patience.

FOR FURTHER REFLECTION

1. *Are you running with perseverance and patience in your effort to stop nibbling?*
2. *Have you been expecting instant results?*
3. *Runners have to find their correct pace. Have you found yours?*

PRAYER

God, I want to run. Teach me how to walk first. Amen

Send in the Clowns

Then our mouth was filled with laughter,
and our tongue with shouts of joy;
then it was said among the nations,
"The Lord has done great things for them."
—Psalm 126:2

Today I saw a television commercial featuring several thousand roosters: just before dawn, they rushed up out of subways, stepped down from trains, and converged onto a city square. As the sun rose, they craned their necks, opened their beaks, and announced the morning in a world-shaking cock-a-doodle. The commercial was so unexpected, so filled with delight, that for a moment, I forgot everything else and gave myself up to laughter.

The rest of that day, my body and soul reflected the benefits of that laughter. God endowed human beings with the ability to respond to humor, improbable situations, and silliness. Clowns are more popular than trapeze artists, and most people would rather see comedy than tragic drama.

Maybe I don't need those potato chips. Maybe I'm just longing for another good laugh.

FOR FURTHER REFLECTION

1. *When did you last have a really hearty laugh?*
2. *How many times during an average day do you smile?*
3. *What can you do to bring more joy and humor into your life?*

PRAYER

Send in the clowns, God. You gave us the gift of laughter;
now help me use it. Amen

In the Shadows

Therefore justice is far from us,
and righteousness does not reach us;
we wait for light, and lo! there is darkness;
and for brightness, but we walk in gloom.

—Isaiah 59:9

I remember a time when I lived in deep shadows. In those days, I was a too-thin young woman with a poor appetite. My marriage was desperately unhappy, my work wasn't going well, and I felt inadequate as a mother. To compound the problem, I had fierce allergies and one case of pneumonia after another.

Shadows aren't always easy to come out of when you have created them yourself. You can't step out of darkness if you're holding onto it like a balloon; it follows you everywhere. What I had to do was let go of the string, turn my face to the sun, and celebrate life.

I'm no longer thin, and my appetite is robust—but I think I'm creating some shadows around myself. I've become so preoccupied with my eating problem that I often feel depressed about it. Food is not my enemy, and eating (or not eating) shouldn't become the most important thing in my life.

FOR FURTHER REFLECTION

Have your eating habits begun to take too big a place in your life? Are you preoccupied with food, calories, diets, and hunger? Take a whole day just to be you. Eat what you want, go someplace, see other people. You'll be refreshed enough to get back on your program.

PRAYER

Let me walk in the light of Your countenance, Lord. Amen

Too Tired?

You shall say to them, Thus says the Lord:
When people fall, do they not get up again?
If they go astray, do they not turn back?
                                        —Jeremiah 8:4

The late television host Dave Garroway was with his five-year-old son in a hotel room at the shore; he was trying to cope with his wife's untimely death. The little boy was bored and restless, and he said to Garroway, "Daddy? Come out and walk on the beach with me."

Garroway shook his head and the child pleaded.

"I can't son," he told the boy. "I'm just too tired."

The little boy sat on the edge of the bed awhile, and then said, "Daddy? Will you just come walk with me till you fall down?"

All God is asking me to do is walk until I fall down. And when I do, God will gently set me on my feet again. No matter what I'm trying, including controlling my eating, failure is only momentary and then grace abounds.

FOR FURTHER REFLECTION

1. *Do you "walk" as far as you can—or do you give up before you start?*
2. *Do you trust God to lift you up when you fall?*
3. *How can you take the first steps?*

PRAYER

Heavenly Father, thank You for picking me up when I fall. Amen

Jacob's Ladder

And he dreamed that there was a ladder
set up on the earth, the top of it reaching to heaven;
and the angels of God were ascending and descending on it.
—Genesis 28:12

When I was a young girl, my friends and I liked to make a Jacob's Ladder with string; it was a game similar to Cat's Cradle, where we manipulated the string until it formed a ladder shape. We had speed contests, and often stood on the school playground in little groups, staring down at our hands as we raced through the activity.

If angels climbed our Jacob's Ladders, we didn't see them; but we read about them in our Sunday School classes, and I had a strong picture in my mind. I believed—and so did most of my friends—that guardian angels surrounded us all the time and kept us from harm.

Do I still have a guardian angel? And is that protector trying desperately to keep me away from foods that are unhealthy? Was it an angel's hand that made me drop the butter on the floor last night?

FOR FURTHER REFLECTION

1. *Do you believe God's angels are protecting you from harm?*
2. *Are you paying attention to your guardian's efforts?*
3. *How involved do you think God is in your nibbling problem?*

PRAYER

Angel of God, my guardian dear,
Committed by God to watch over me here;
Ever this day, be at my side
To lead, to love, to guard and to guide. Amen

The River

There is a river whose streams make glad the city of God,
the holy habitation of the Most High.

—Psalm 46:4

We lived for ten years in a small beach town south of San Diego. The Tijuana River divided our beach from Mexico's. Sometimes when the tide was out, the river was so narrow you could step over it—which is what I saw someone do one day.

I basked on the sand, watching a Hispanic man on the Mexican side, using a surveyor's transit. He looked, measured, made notes, then backed up and repeated the process. Finally, he stepped over the river, went through his routine one more time, then folded up his transit and got into a waiting car. Only then did I realize that he had probably crossed illegally into the United States.

In those days our immigration laws weren't so fierce. That man, wearing jeans and a T-shirt, wasn't a Coyote, who smuggles people over the border, or a drug runner carrying a million dollars' worth of heroin. He was probably just a person looking for freedom. And so am I. I want freedom from food.

FOR FURTHER REFLECTION

In your journal, write a paragraph or two about what your life would be like if you were free from overeating. Then make a list of things you need to "step over" to achieve that freedom.

PRAYER

Set me free, gracious Lord;
help me cross into a country where I don't overeat. Amen

Fifth Circle of Hell

All things are wearisome;
more than one can express;
the eye is not satisfied with seeing,
or the ear filled with hearing.

—Ecclesiastes 1:8

In Dante's *Inferno,* written in the early 1300s, his guide takes him to the Fifth Circle of Hell, to see those who were guilty of the deadly sin of sloth. There, people lay in cold black mire, longing for another chance on earth. No fires, no pitchforks, no red-suited underdevils, hurling coal or wood into the mammoth furnace. This part of hell is a cold place where nothing will ever happen.

Sloth isn't the kind of laziness that keeps you from cleaning out the garage or taking a two-mile run. Sloth, or indolence, is a spiritual apathy, torpor, hopelessness—a failure to care or act. An Anglican bishop described it as something that would make you cynical about everything—*if* you had the energy.

I think my nibbling rises out of sloth, out of thinking "Oh, what's the use?" or "I don't care." But if the body is the temple of God, am I chipping away at the temple's marble columns with my eating? And do I care enough to stop it?

FOR FURTHER REFLECTION

1. *Do you ever fall into the deadly sin of sloth?*
2. *Do you lack passion in your life?*
3. *Can you, with God's help, get out of this fifth circle?*

PRAYER

O God, save me from the cold mud of slothfulness.
When I am apathetic, teach me joy. Amen

Celebration

And get the fatted calf and kill it,
and let us eat and celebrate.

—Luke 15:23

Three Dog Night, a rock-and-roll group from the early seventies, called us to celebrate and to dance to the music. I'm really a celebration person, but the problem is that most festive occasions involve food. At our church, every time there's a baptism, a birthday, a wedding, or even a funeral, we have a reception with all kinds of food offerings. Sandwiches, deviled eggs, potato and macaroni salads, tarts, cookies, cake, and pie all appear on our decorated buffet tables, and we're always happy to serve up some good, sweet punch.

And almost every other celebration in my family or among my friends involves a festive dinner. My writers' critique group meets for breakfast, and when I want to visit with a friend, we meet for lunch at a favorite restaurant.

I can't stay home from church events just to avoid food, and I don't really want to put a stop to the other occasions. What I've got to do is quit nibbling in between celebrations and make sensible selections when I'm at them.

FOR FURTHER REFLECTION

1. *Do you feel compelled to eat at every celebration?*
2. *Could you have a good time at a party without eating anything unhealthy?*
3. *What other ways can you think of to celebrate important events?*

PRAYER

Loving Father, teach me how to participate
in celebrations without overindulging. Amen

The First Steps

For you need endurance,
so that when you have done the will of God,
you may receive what was promised.
—Hebrews 10:36

I taught piano for more than thirty years. I often told my students not to return to the beginning every time they made a mistake, but to correct it and go on. "If you fall over a rock when you leave here, would you come clear back to the piano and set out again?" I asked.

A couple of months ago I took my first steps in my effort to quit overeating. And I took them again in a week. And again. And again. I keep starting over because I keep falling over rocks, sneaking a cupcake or going on an all-out feast.

But I don't need to keep telling myself to start over; in fact, I need to keep going. If I look back to when I began to curtail my nibbling, I realize I am at least eating a lot less, and I'm making progress.

I don't have to go clear back to the piano every time I fall over a rock.

FOR FURTHER REFLECTION

1. *How much time have you spent making fresh starts?*
2. *Have you actually made some progress in your eating program?*
3. *How does knowing this help you persevere?*

PRAYER

Guide my steps, Lord, and help me resume after I fall. Amen

Who Am I?

*Then the Lord God formed man
from the dust of the ground,
and breathed into his nostrils the breath of life;
and the man became a living being.*
—Genesis 2:7

A synergism is something that's more than the sum total of its parts. People are synergistic: they're certainly more than just their physical parts. Joseph Wood Krutch, the late naturalist, said in his book *The Great Chain of Life,* "If man is no more than an improbable set of chemical reactions . . . that these reactions should trace themselves back to their own origins is a staggering supposition."

But which of my origins is really me? My ancestors' genes, or the major influences in my childhood, or the total of my life experiences? Certainly, all of those elements contributed to who I am and why I behave as I do. But the real source of my life is beyond earthly experience or genetic combinations. I am a child of *God.*

The part of me that nibbles probably comes from ancestry and experience. But the brave, strong woman inside me is spiritual, and I think she can stop the rest of me.

FOR FURTHER REFLECTION

Read Romans 7:15 through 8:2 and then make a list of the qualities you find in your spiritual self.

PRAYER

*Please, God, show me the center of myself,
the part that comes from You,
and help me live from that center. Amen*

Surrender

He said, "Then put away the foreign gods that are among you,
and incline your hearts to the Lord, the God of Israel."
—Joshua 24:23

God isn't trying to break my will, but to refine it. God wants to take the coarse burlap of my resolve, and turn it into satin. But surrender is both the hardest and the easiest thing for humans to do. You can agonize for weeks or months about a decision; you can even convince yourself that both choices are really from God. When I go through that process and finally turn God's way, the feeling of relief is palpable and I think, "Why didn't I do this before? It was so easy!"

It's a stacked deck: God will win, regardless of my recalcitrance, and when God wins, so do I. Because the Lord ultimately has my good in mind. So how does this affect my overeating, my snacking and nibbling?

Well, I can go on rationalizing that I don't *really* eat that much and that my nibbling is just my eating style. (Of course, what I don't always admit is that what I snack on is rarely fruit or raw vegetables, and that mine is the hand most often in the cookie jar.) Or I can say, "Okay God."

FOR FURTHER REFLECTION

1. *Do you resist God in your daily life?*
2. *How do you make decisions—with or without prayer?*
3. *What is your reaction when you surrender to God?*

PRAYER

Eternal God, You delight in my surrender.
Give me the insight to know Your will. Amen

Not Magic

One does not live by bread alone,
but by every word that comes from the mouth of God.
—Matthew 4:4

In fairy tales, wizards and magicians always have plenty of thunder, fire, lightning, hurricanes, dragons, gnomes, and powerful potions at their disposal.

Jesus was not a wizard. Instead of hurling lightning bolts or manifesting a fire-breathing creature out of the air, He took a sheet of matzoh off the table, broke it, and passed it around the room to His followers, murmuring, "This is my body." There were no thunder crashes, no treble choirs, no wizardry of any kind. What Jesus offered was not magical, but holy; not illusionary, but perhaps the realest object since creation. Plain unleavened Passover bread, sanctified by the words "Blessed are you, Lord God, King of the Universe, for You bring bread from the earth."

The gift of life is sent to us not by sorcery and magic, but by the power of God. And the gift of food is always holy when two or three of us are gathered together. Maybe nibbling—because so often it's done alone and furtively, and without a blessing—is an attempt to be more magical than holy.

FOR FURTHER REFLECTION

It's easy to become a "magical thinker," pretending to yourself that you aren't overeating, or that nibbling can't really make you fat or unhealthy. Today, ask God about your magical thinking, and journal what you hear in answer.

PRAYER

Thank You, Lord Jesus, for being a Savior
instead of a sorcerer. Amen

The Sheep of God's Hand

For he is our God, and we are the people of his pasture, and the sheep of his hand. O that today you would listen to his voice!
—Psalm 95:7

We once owned a lamb who shied from physical connection with us. We fed her every day, but she ran when she saw us coming, and if while she was munching grain from the manger we reached out to caress her woolly head, she bolted. She actually preferred the company of my son's seventeen-hand thoroughbred horse, and often grazed standing under him. The first time we had her sheared it took us nearly an hour to capture her, throw a burlap sack over her head, and lead her to the shearing shed. We wanted the best for her, but she didn't know that.

It wasn't until we had that crazy antisocial lamb that I realized that to be the sheep of Christ's hand means being *willing* to be carried by the Good Shepherd. He wants what's best for me, but sometimes I run away when I see Him coming. Am I standing under the tall "horse" of overeating to resist God?

FOR FURTHER REFLECTION

1. Can you imagine yourself as one of God's lambs?
2. Do you let God love you, or do you run away?
3. Is your overeating a form of running from God?

PRAYER

I know You love me, Lord.
Help me to run toward You. Amen

The Berlin Wall

And the wall of the city will fall down flat,
and all the people shall charge straight ahead.
—Joshua 6:5

I was watching a movie when a newsbreak interrupted, showing East Germans coming through the Berlin Wall without interference from the guards. Soon the wall started coming down: first people took small pieces, then bigger chunks, and finally, tanks razed the structure. For several decades, that wall that represented tyranny had been the site of death and despair; and then it was gone.

I have to remember to look at my issues with food the same way. If I start to tear down the wall of self-destruction within me, faithfully undertaking one tiny piece of it at a time, God will raze the rest of that wall for me. My task is to *start* the demolition process.

FOR FURTHER REFLECTION

1. *What first steps* away *from overeating can you take?*
2. *Which small behavior will you change first?*
3. *How can you help yourself remember that God is in this?*

PRAYER

You made the walls fall in Jericho and Berlin, God,
when people listened to You. I'm listening:
tell me where to start breaking down the stubborn wall inside me.
Amen

True Freedom

I shall walk at liberty,
for I have sought your precepts.

—Psalm 119:45

Praising the Law, the psalmist speaks of the kind of freedom that comes only with obedience. The last verse of Psalm 119 says, "I have gone astray like a lost sheep; seek out your servant, for I do not forget your commandments," which reminds me that the Lord is my shepherd. An animal that wanders off alone isn't really free: it has to spend all its time watching for predators or hunting for food. Sheep that stay in the flock and follow their shepherd are free to eat better food, sleep, and gambol in safety.

But the psalm also reminds us that lost sheep don't look for their shepherd; it's up to him to find them and take them home. Pictures of the Good Shepherd show Him carrying a lamb or sheep on His shoulders, and holding the animal's feet so it can't fall.

So when I get lost in any aspect of my life, God goes on a hunt and brings me back to where I can be myself. And knowing that God will never let me go is true freedom.

FOR FURTHER REFLECTION

1. *Do you see following a sensible dietary regimen as an infringement on your freedom?*
2. *Could it actually be a way toward greater freedom?*

PRAYER

Your path is safe, and Your leadership
is designed to set me free, God. Amen

The Wild Rose

My child, keep my words
and store up my commandments with you.

—Proverbs 7:1

Wild pink roses tumble over our hillsides in spring, scenting the air and calling bees out of their hives. In the fall those same rosebushes bear bright red rose hips, full of nutrients for the rosebush, seeds for more roses—and the makings of wonderful jelly.

The rose flower stores up energy from the sun and rain and by summer's end, it begins to form the firm round "rose apples" whose fragrance always makes me think of autumn.

That rose hip jelly is loaded with vitamin C, so it's healthy for me to eat—in moderation. The whole trick to changing my nibbling habit is in enjoyment: savoring that product of sun and rain, inhaling its perfume, letting it rest on my tongue long enough to make me imagine a roomful of roses, slowly consuming its delights.

A rose is God's way of making another rose. In the same way, I am God's way of making another me. An eternal one.

FOR FURTHER REFLECTION

When you're eating, do you appreciate the food's origins, its fragrance, and its delicious taste—or do you gobble it down in order to take another bite? If so, how can you change that?

PRAYER

Dear Lord, Give me the ability to taste and smell the beauty and bounty around me. Amen

Body Prayer

At the name of Jesus every knee should bend,
in heaven and on earth and under the earth.

—Philippians 2:10

I was on a 747 rushing toward Israel. I slept badly and as we flew into the dawn I woke to see an elderly Jewish man, clad in black coat and hat, his white earlocks bobbing as he stood at the window, his hands raised, his body bending over and over in one devout bow after another as he performed his morning praise to God. He was absorbed in adoration, totally caught up in his worship, alone with the King of the Universe, translating his love for God into movement, ignoring the more than two hundred other people on the plane.

"Body prayer" is an important form of worship. So when I pray at home, I kneel, or I stand like the man on the plane, with my hands raised; and when I sing the name of Jesus in a hymn, I try to remember to bend my knee.

One more way to pray with my body is to avoid putting unnecessary food into it.

FOR FURTHER REFLECTION

1. *Are you physically, mentally, and emotionally reverent to God?*
2. *How does overeating suggest irreverence?*
3. *What can you change about your physical worship?*

PRAYER

I worship and love You, Lord God,
and I will try to show more reverence. Amen

Slippery Slope

He will not let your foot be moved;
he who keeps you will not slumber.

—Psalm 121:3

I was almost up the mountain when the rain began to pour. I could no longer get a firm handhold, and the dirt on the slope turned into a slurry. I slid downward for a terrifying fifty feet. I was saved by a bush, and I was hoisted back up by my companions above me and the rope line I had clipped to my waistband.

Now, whenever I hear a lawyer or pundit say "slippery slope," a favorite legal and political term, I know what they're talking about. If I had been climbing alone, even the bush couldn't have held me forever. I would have slid down into a great pile of broken rock and been seriously injured or even killed, and I was grateful for help.

The moral is that when you climb mountains, you shouldn't do it alone. I could never climb the mountain of changing my eating without support, either. I have good friends, a husband, and God, all working for me. And God always hoists me up when I slip. Now, if I can just get a foothold . . .

FOR FURTHER REFLECTION

1. *Do you slip often in your "climb" to stop nibbling?*
2. *Who keeps you from sliding all the way?*
3. *Are you grateful for that help?*

PRAYER

Thank You, God, for the many times
You have kept me from slipping into danger. Amen

Keeping the Faith

Since, then, we have a great high priest
who has passed through the heavens, Jesus, the Son of God,
let us hold fast to our confession.

—Hebrews 4:14

Some may find it difficult to believe in an "invisible" God. Although it may be natural to seek out evidence before committing to a belief, the Bible says in Hebrews 11:1 that faith is being sure of what we hope for and certain of what we do *not* see.

God promised me eternal life, and I promised myself that I'd quit overeating. So although I can't see either heaven or how thin I'm going to get, a promise is a promise, as kids like to say, and I have to believe in God and keep faith with myself, too.

Actually, when I think about it, both those promises involve God. I can't get to heaven or quit overeating *or* keep the faith without God's grace.

FOR FURTHER REFLECTION

1. *Do you call on God's grace to keep your faith alive?*
2. *Do you ask for grace to keep from nibbling?*
3. *What do you need to do to bolster your faith?*

PRAYER

Grant me the grace, Lord, to keep the faith. Amen

The Secret of the Calendar

Three times in the year you shall hold a festival for me. . . .
observe the festival of unleavened bread . . .
observe the festival of harvest . . .
observe the festival of ingathering at the end of the year . . .
—Exodus 23:14-16

I once worked in a beautiful music store with pigskin floors and sculptured walls. My desk faced a wall carved to look like the circular Mayan calendar, that mysterious timekeeper whose dates extend into this century, even though the culture that created it is gone.

Every calendar has this secret: time is important to God. He gave the Jews holy *times*: the Sabbath, the Passover, and other feasts and festivals that the devout still celebrate. We Christians celebrate Christmas wherever we are—in snowy climes, in the desert, or the jungle. Easter happens in our hearts, houses, and churches. We tell God, "Our times are in your hand."

We aren't sure about the location of Calvary, and we've failed to find the Ark of the Covenant. Why? Perhaps because God doesn't want us to put our faith in places or things, but to take charge of our time.

FOR FURTHER REFLECTION

Consider how you will spend today.

PRAYER

Eternal God, show me how best to spend my precious hours. Amen

Narcissus

Woe to you, scribes and Pharisees, hypocrites!
For you clean the outside of the cup and of the plate,
but inside they are full of greed and self-indulgence.
—Matthew 23:25

Narcissus was a beautiful lad in Greek mythology, who had never seen his own face until the day he knelt to drink from a deep pool. He didn't realize what he saw was a reflection, and he fell in love with his own image. He couldn't leave, and one ending of the story has him take root and turn into a beautiful lily, the narcissus. Another ending says he bent to kiss his own lips, and fell into the pool and drowned; then the gods took pity and let him return as the beautiful lily.

A narcissist is a person whose world is seen through his or her own beautiful reflection. In negative narcissism, people see life in terms of their own unworthiness and unlovability. A *negative* narcissist can become anorexic or extremely obese, an alcoholic or a drug addict.

So while I'm working on my nibbling, it's also important for me to live life, go to church, see friends, reach out to others, and enjoy my work. Or I might become a solitary lily by a pond.

FOR FURTHER REFLECTION

1. *How much time do you spend thinking about your own failings?*
2. *What do you need to do to look outside yourself?*
3. *Where is God in this?*

PRAYER

Dear God, save me from myself.
Set my sights on You, and on service to others. Amen

On the Wings of Eagles

As an eagle stirs up its nest, and hovers over its young;
as it spreads its wings, takes them up,
and bears them aloft on its pinions . . .

—Deuteronomy 32:11

When eagle chicks are old enough to fledge, their parents begin ripping up the nest. With their beaks, they tear out the material they once spent so long collecting, and leave the fledglings no nest to hide in. Then they push them off the cliff. But they haven't abandoned their children: they immediately swoop down below their chicks, catch them on their powerful wings, then take them back to the ledge. Over and over. This is how they teach the chicks their most basic survival skill: flight. Eagles must fly, both to eat and to escape danger.

God regularly forces me out of my cozy lifestyle, out to the edge, then pushes me off. But instead of letting me fall to earth and die, God constantly rushes out and catches me on those sacred pinions. So if I fail today to change my eating habits, God will take me back to the ledge and we'll keep working until I can soar.

FOR FURTHER REFLECTION

1. *Is God pushing you to the edge of your comfort level?*
2. *Do you experience terror as you fall?*
3. *Can you trust God to catch you?*

PRAYER

Teach me trust, God, so that while I am learning to fly,
I depend on Your strength. Amen

Red Carpet

For with you is the fountain of life;
in your light we see light.

—Psalm 36:9

At the Peabody Hotel in Memphis, Tennessee, someone rolls out a red carpet from the elevator to the fountain every evening at five. The elevator door opens and out waddles a row of ducks, who tramp to the fountain and enjoy an evening swim. When they get out they preen their feathers and shake, then head back into the elevator, where an employee of the hotel takes them to their room—presumably a place considered luxurious by ducks—for dinner and sleep. I understand that the ducks at the Peabody Hotel are treated with great deference and pampered with the finest of duck foods in their suite.

Sometimes my husband and I sit in separate rooms, watching television while we eat. If I'm working on deadline, I eat at my desk. If my husband is away, supper may be eaten in front of the refrigerator. And when I eat without ceremony like that I always feel hungry later and start nibbling. But God is beckoning down a red carpet, so tonight we're eating on good china, with lighted candles, near the fountain of God's love.

FOR FURTHER REFLECTION

1. *Do you make mealtimes festive and gracious?*
2. *Does the way you have dinner say something about your self-esteem?*
3. *How can you make your meals reflect God's presence?*

PRAYER

Help me, Lord, to appreciate the food you've blessed me with and to dine with dignity. Amen

A Time to Throw Away Stones

For everything there is a season,
and a time for every matter under heaven . . .
a time to throw away stones,
and a time to gather stones together . . .
—Ecclesiastes 3:1, 5

When Solomon spoke of gathering and throwing away stones, he was reminding us of the silliness of life's work. You pick up rocks, you throw down rocks. The sun rises and sets, he says, life is just one thing after another.

How did Solomon become so depressed? He had everything: a palace, riches, fame, wives, and wisdom. Every time I read Ecclesiastes my one thought is, "Boy, does this guy need Jesus!" No matter how much money or bliss or earthly authority you have, *nothing* is enough unless you know the Redeemer.

Job, though he was broken down in every way imaginable, and was deprived of children, money, and health, said, "For I know that my Redeemer lives, and that at the last he will stand upon the earth; and after my skin has been thus destroyed, then in my flesh I shall see God, whom I shall see on my side, and my eyes shall behold, and not another." Perhaps deprivation makes you more likely to celebrate.

Then maybe I better start praising the Lord. I miss all those snacks I've been "deprived" of, but I know that my Redeemer lives.

FOR FURTHER REFLECTION

Do you ever feel completely defeated in your effort to quit nibbling? Despair is the Enemy's favorite weapon! Make a list in your journal of the blessings God has given you.

PRAYER

Merciful Lord, You have redeemed me.
What more can I possibly need? Amen

Good News

The Lord sets the prisoners free.

—Psalm 146:7

My friend DeLora was asked if she'd visit the women in the Las Vegas jail. On the first Sunday the matron flung open the door to a large room surrounded by cells, hollered, "Preacher's here," and left. DeLora, a petite woman, was terrified. She murmured, "Well, I'm not a preacher," but nobody answered. She sat down and said to the shadowy figures behind their cell bars, "Would anyone like to come read the Bible and pray with me?" She issued the invitation several times and was about to leave when a young prostitute tiptoed out, weeping. "I need help!" the girl cried. "God loves you," my friend told her. Eventually, every woman in the jail came into the room to hear the Good News. My friend's ministry at that institution lasted eighteen years.

Sometimes I feel like a prisoner of food, waiting for a DeLora to come into my life. But good news is as close as my Bible, and if I read it and pray, I can break free.

FOR FURTHER REFLECTION

Do you ever feel imprisoned by your eating habits? Try to think about something else for a few minutes. Each day, extend that time, so that in a month you're able to go a long time without letting food or your problems with food enter your mind.

PRAYER

I need to hear good news, Lord.
The news that I'm free. Amen

Only Human

The spirit of God has made me,
and the breath of the Almighty gives me life.

—Job 33:4

I told a close friend that after several weeks of progress, I had spent a whole afternoon and evening stuffing food into my mouth. "Well," she said, "you're only human, after all."

She was being kind, but she was wrong. I'm not *only* human. You might think I'm just a middle-aged lady with curly blond hair, but I'm not *just* anything. I have divine breath within me. God has promised me eternal life, so I'm an immortal being. And immortal beings shouldn't be consumed with overeating.

I know what Paul meant about the war in his members, and what the writer of Hebrews intended when he wrote about the Word of God dividing soul and spirit. My soul, the combination of my temperament, emotions, and mind, is always fighting with the divine spirit within me, especially when it comes to nibbling. Fortunately, the breath of God is stronger.

FOR FURTHER REFLECTION

1. *What is running your life: your human self, or your spirit?*
2. *How does knowing you have God's breath within you affect your eating?*

PRAYER

I heartily thank You, dear God,
for the breath of life and for Your Spirit within me. Amen

Home from Oz

Where can I go from your spirit?
Or where can I flee from your presence?
If I ascend to heaven, you are there;
if I make my bed in Sheol, you are there.

—Psalm 139:7, 8

When I get to heaven, I think I'll look back at life on earth as if it were a bizarre dream, where everything is out of order, where movement and communication are chaotic, and craziness reigns, just as it did when Dorothy visited Oz. Instead of wicked witches, flowers that knock you out, and vengeful flying monkeys, I'll remember wars, school shootings, and stock market manipulation. And instead of clicking magic red slippers to go home, I have to go through the hard adventure of death.

But God didn't put me on earth just to die, so while I'm here, I want to face the last half of my life with grace and humor and charity. I hope to contribute care for the planet, to have love for my fellow Oz dwellers, and to show kindness in every situation.

Oh, and I want to keep my body in good order to be resurrected, so I'll have to eat the way God designed me to eat.

FOR FURTHER REFLECTION

Living on earth is chaos, full of sorrow and tragedy, but offering moments of great joy and satisfaction. Make a list of things you would like to accomplish on earth; include overcoming your overeating if that's a desire of yours.

PRAYER

Lord God, I look forward to the day I can see You face to face.
Until then grant me the grace and strength to live fully
and to contribute to life around me. Amen

Passive Voice

Therefore prepare your minds for action;
discipline yourselves; set all your hope on the grace
that Jesus Christ will bring you when he is revealed.
—1 Peter 1:13

Passive voice is a way of writing and speaking in which people are acted upon. Look at this statement in passive voice: "X-rays were taken, and a painkiller was administered to Bill." Poor Bill! He was either unconscious, or had decided not to say a word about what was done to him. To get Bill back in charge of himself, you could say, "Bill went for chest x-rays, and asked the nurse for a painkiller."

Editors tell writers that using passive voice makes for weak writing. Well, *living* in passive voice makes for weak living. Some people live their lives as the objects of action, rather than acting, and they make excuses for themselves. "Passive aggressive" is the psychologist's term for a person who controls others by doing nothing, by procrastination and stubbornness.

But is that any way to live? Isn't it better to say, "I am, I do, I will," than to pretend to myself that I have no power over my own life? Of course, this means I have to take charge of my own overeating, doesn't it?

FOR FURTHER REFLECTION

1. *Do you take responsibility for your own actions?*
2. *Who is in charge of your eating?*
3. *What changes do you need to make in your attitude about action versus passivity?*

PRAYER

You are my guide and my director, God;
grant me the degree of self-direction I need. Amen

Planning Consultant

And the twelve gates are twelve pearls,
each of the gates is a single pearl,
and the street of the city is pure gold, transparent as glass.
—Revelation 21:21

You can't carve or flatten or shape a pearl. A pearl is an organic gem, created when an oyster covers a foreign object with layer after layer of translucent nacre. So if each of the twelve gates of the City of God, where the Lamb is the light, is made from an immense pearl, God must have started culturing some super-oysters somewhere in the ocean long, long ago. He had to start at the Beginning to plan for the End.

I need God to be my planning consultant. Instead of remembering that the big slice of pizza I'm eating will soon show up on my thighs, I see only what I want to see at the moment. When the urge for chips and dip or fast food or ice cream hits me, I don't stop to think that as a result I'll have heartburn, or gain weight, or feel guilty afterward; I just listen to my taste buds, calling for more.

FOR FURTHER REFLECTION

1. *Are you so locked into what you want that you ignore results?*
2. *How can you plan better than that?*
3. *What will you use to remind yourself?*

PRAYER

Lord, be my planning consultant.
When I start to nibble, please speak loudly
to remind me of the consequences. Amen

God's Works

Great are the works of the Lord,
studied by all who delight in them.

—Psalm 111:2

"I know only two kinds of birds," a man said at the church coffee hour. "Crows and robins. That's plenty."

Actually, the birds the man was calling "crows" are Pacific Northwest ravens, but I'm glad he recognized at least two of God's finest creations. I'm just sorry he doesn't see fat gray bushtits nesting in blackberry brambles, and rosy finches gathering on patios and around chimneys. He ignores pine siskins and the hundreds of Canada geese that winter here, and the piñon and Steller's jays, whose blue feathers almost match the sky.

You have to delight in God's works to study them. After talking to him awhile, I knew this man could have been in the Gobi desert for all he cared about our birds, our deer, our mountain lilacs, and wild pink rhododendrons.

I'm one of God's works, too. But is my self-image so wounded that I can't see myself that way? Am I as blind as that man, unable to see the beauty of all of God's creation, myself included?

FOR FURTHER REFLECTION

1. *Do you consider yourself as valuable as birds, trees, and flowers?*
2. *What does Scripture say about your being precious to God?*
3. *Do you have a right to value yourself less than God values you?*

PRAYER

You made everything, God, including me.
Show me how I look to You. Amen

God's Gifts

Every generous act of giving, with every perfect gift,
is from above, coming down from the Father of lights,
with whom there is no variation or shadow due to change.

—James 1:17

I once gave a small grandson a little camera for Christmas. He took pictures of everything, without regard to the amount of light. He pulled out the film and played with it as if it were an accordion. He left the camera on the lawn; when the sprinklers came on, it was ruined. The fault wasn't his—it was mine. I shouldn't have given such a young child such a grown-up gift.

But is it God's fault that I misuse the gift of food? Am I too young or dumb to make intelligent choices about what (and how much) I eat? Well, of course not. I'm a grown woman, able to make good choices about food and sleep and everything vital to my life.

My grandson is now really interested in photography, so I may give him another camera. And God keeps putting plenty of good, healthy food in front of me, trusting me to use His gifts the right way.

FOR FURTHER REFLECTION

Write down a list of God's gifts in your life. Then make another list of things God has deprived you of. Which list is longer? Which is the most honest?

PRAYER

Thank you, most gracious God, for the many
wonderful gifts You have showered down upon me,
including the gifts of life and salvation through Jesus Christ. Amen

Magic v. Mercy

Stand fast in your enchantments and your many sorceries . . .
See, they are like stubble, the fire consumes them . . .
—Isaiah 47:12, 14

My friend complains that she's been praying for two years for her husband to get a job. She thinks God is saying no to her pleas without a good reason. "God says no just to frustrate me," she insists. She—in fact most of us—would probably like it better if God would simply "fix" all the troubles in the world, including unemployment, divorce, famine, war, and illness. In fact, why can't God create little miracles that would keep a dish from breaking when it falls, and retrieve keys that you locked in the car?

The problem is, we would have to sacrifice free will for that kind of magic. God may be telling ten companies to hire my friend's husband, but personnel directors have free will and can disobey God's orders. And God won't defy his own physical laws to keep the falling saucer from hitting the hard floor.

Would I trade my individuality and free will for magic? No thanks. Even though real life is complicated, I don't want to be a puppet with no will or creativity. So I pray for help to overcome my nibbling, but ultimately I get to do the hard work.

FOR FURTHER REFLECTION

1. *Do you expect magic in your life?*
2. *Can you forgive others for misusing their free will?*
3. *Can you learn to use yours wisely?*

PRAYER

God of the Universe, You gave me intelligence
and free will. Help me use them wisely. Amen

Trying to Forgive

Lord, if another member of the church sins against me,
how often should I forgive? As many as seven times?
—Matthew 18:21

God expects me to yield up all old grudges, to respond with love to slights and hurts, and to bless my enemies. I don't have many enemies to bless. I spend so much time alone, writing, that I cherish the few friends I have time for, and I can shrug off people who might dislike me. But I do have an enemy: the past. Pain from the past occasionally pops up. On nights when I find it hard to sleep, I replay old scenes with my mother or with friends who have betrayed me, and I come close to tears. And then what do I do? You're right: I get up and eat.

I have two tasks now. The first is to remember those painful moments and forgive the people in them, and to keep in mind that my memory may be distorted. And the second task is to find a better cure for past unhappiness than food.

FOR FURTHER REFLECTION

Make a list of people who hurt you, and painful situations from the past. Light a candle, then name each person aloud who hurt you, adding the words "I forgive you." Burn the list with the candle flame, then offer a prayer of thanks to God.

PRAYER

Lord Jesus, You taught us to forgive that we
might be forgiven. Grant me now the strength
to bless all those people who have
wounded me in the past. Amen

Clematis

Turn again, O God of hosts;
look down from heaven, and see; have regard for this vine,
the stock that your right hand planted.

—Psalm 80:14, 15

A bedraggled clematis vine on my patio wall has never flowered. A practical gardener might pull out the plant and throw it away. But I've invested too much time and effort in that vine, and as I prune and fertilize, I have faith that one day—maybe next spring—I'll see it bursting into brilliant lavender blossom.

Sometimes I'm probably as hard a trial to God as that clematis vine is to me. I haven't blossomed yet as a more sensible eater, and I'm still lagging behind in many other areas. If I were a vine, would the Master Gardener dig me out and throw me on the burn pile or compost heap? Would the One who planted me consider "the stock that [His] right hand planted"?

God is stubborn, and will keep nurturing me with love until the day I achieve my potential. The rest of the world may someday give up on me, but God believes in what He has planted.

FOR FURTHER REFLECTION

1. *If God never gives up, will you persevere as well?*
2. *What is the major block to your "blossoming"?*
3. *How can you help yourself while God helps you?*

PRAYER

God, You are the gardener of my soul.
Help me to know Your plan,
to grow strong, and to flower. Amen

Clean Your Plate

And all ate and were filled;
and they took up what was left over
of the broken pieces, twelve baskets full.
—Matthew 14:20

My husband came from a clean-your-plate family, with a harsh father who measured out some heavy discipline to children who left food on their plates or sneaked food between meals. He said his childhood was punctuated by instances of being either over-full or faint with hunger. I was a thin, allergic child who couldn't have milk, wheat, many vegetables, or any citrus fruit, and I didn't have much appetite. So my parents were delighted when I ate *anything*, whether it was at meals or in between.

That early training affected the way we each see food. My husband eats large portions at two or three meals, whereas I eat small meals and graze all day. Well, my husband is severely overweight and has late-onset diabetes. So maybe nibbling isn't so bad; maybe it's *what* I nibble that needs to change. I need to give myself permission to eat all the fresh fruit and vegetables and low-fat yogurt I want, and give myself some credit for avoiding french fries, chocolate, and sugary drinks.

FOR FURTHER REFLECTION

1. *What ideas about food did you grow up with?*
2. *How do they affect your eating habits?*
3. *How can you translate your food beliefs into healthy living?*

PRAYER

Lord God, instill in me the habits You want me to have. Amen

Trigger Locks

You shall eat your bread to the full,
and live securely in your land.

—Leviticus 26:5

My gun-collecting neighbor has children, so he's put trigger locks on all his guns. They're also secured in a childproof gun cabinet, all unloaded and broken down. That neighbor has gone to impressive lengths to prevent his children from getting into his weapons.

I've seen pictures of ropes or chains around refrigerators, and I've even heard of refrigerator locks. But to keep me from ever nibbling, you'd have to put a lock on every cupboard, cracker jar, and potato chip sack in my kitchen. Or put me inside a bubble room where no food is available.

What I need is a trigger lock on my appetite, and that has to come from inside me. I'm the only one who can decide not to eat the wrong things at the wrong time. And I can't do it alone: God has to help me. Without God, I'm helpless. With God, I become a powerful person who can do anything. Well, almost anything.

FOR FURTHER REFLECTION

If telling yourself that certain foods are off-limits makes them even more enticing to you, remind yourself that with God's help, you are stronger than the pull of the food.

PRAYER

God, You are my champion, my helper, and my leader.
Protect me from overeating. Amen

Enemy Territory

How could we sing the Lord's song
in a foreign land?

—Psalm 137:4

There is a story of American soldiers interned in a Japanese prison camp during World War II who had to do heavy manual labor. As they did, one of them constantly hummed "America the Beautiful." Soon all the men were humming right under the noses of their captors. They never sang the words aloud, because some of the guards spoke English, but the tune alone gave them courage. When they returned home after the war was over, they said that their humming actually kept them alive under the most terrible of circumstances.

We are in the Enemy's territory. If you don't believe it, watch the news. But Christians work to overthrow the powers of evil. C. S. Lewis said we're holding underground meetings in church, gathering strength for the final battle and the courage to go on. So this evening, instead of raiding the refrigerator or munching on cookies, I sat at the piano and sang my favorite hymns. The Enemy who hopes for my failure had to listen to all that humming instead.

FOR FURTHER REFLECTION

1. *Do you remember that the Enemy wants you to keep overeating?*
2. *Can you also remember that Christ is fighting the battle, too?*
3. *Today, hum your favorite hymns or choruses as you go about your day.*

PRAYER

Save me from the time of trial, Lord,
and deliver me from evil. Amen

Lost World

Your ancient ruins shall be rebuilt;
you shall raise up the foundations of many generations;
you shall be called the repairer of the breach,
the restorer of streets to live in.

—Isaiah 58:12

Inside me is a lost world, a place where life was perfect. The fallen man and woman who were driven from the Garden are an aspect of my personality, and every now and then they voice their longing for home. This desire to return to our roots is not uncommon, even among those who don't believe the Bible story of creation. In fact, even some weight-loss plans tap into the desire, with one popular book featuring the "cave man diet" and another with a plan based on your original ethnicity.

Well, since my ethnicity is mostly Viking, should I don a hat with horns, a long buckskin shirt, and eat the old Scandinavian meal of meat, mead, and lingonberries? I certainly don't think that would take me back to perfection, but I do think the gate to the ancient world is ajar. Once I appropriate the grace of Jesus Christ, bought with His blood, I'm on my way through the gate and heading home—not to a Viking town, but to the place where I can live with God.

And I think I'll have better things than food to think about in heaven. So why not start thinking about them now?

FOR FURTHER REFLECTION

1. *Do you believe that humans have lost both their knowledge and their innocence?*
2. *How would that knowledge change your eating?*
3. *Are you on the way back to God's perfect world?*

PRAYER

Thank You, God, for Your love in sending
Jesus to save and perfect me. Amen

Woman at the Well

The woman said to him, "Sir, give me this water,
so that I may never be thirsty
or have to keep coming here to draw water."

—John 4:15

The woman at the well was dying of thirst. She tried to quench it with men—she'd had five husbands and was living with another man. She very likely hung out with other loose women at taverns. But nothing ever assuaged her thirst until the day Jesus asked her for a drink.

In her book *I Went to the Animal Fair,* Heather Harpham writes about going to the Oregon coast with an unnamed friend whom she calls "She Who is Like a Lion." As they walk along the sand, Heather talks about a man to whom she is attracted, and the "Lion" says, "No matter who the man is, he isn't what you really want. You want God."

I've been restless and vaguely hungry, standing in front of the open refrigerator, eating the skin off a roast chicken or scarfing a piece of pie. I've needed Heather's lion friend to tell me, "Quit eating and go pray. What you want is God."

FOR FURTHER REFLECTION

1. *What are you hungry and thirsty for?*
2. *If you could see God face to face, would you still feel hungry?*
3. *How will you begin to look for God?*

PRAYER

Feed me with Your presence, Lord. Amen

Lobster Quadrille

You have turned my mourning into dancing;
you have taken off my sackcloth and clothed me with joy.
—Psalm 30:11

In the tenth chapter of *Alice in Wonderland*, the Mock Turtle and the Gryphon explain the lobster quadrille to Alice: You take a lobster partner, advancing, circling, then throwing the lobster as far into the sea as possible, swimming after it, turning somersaults, changing to a new lobster, and heading back to land; and then repeating.

When I was a child I read *Alice* over and over. I savored the moment when, while demonstrating the quadrille, the Mock Turtle and the Gryphon sang, "Will you, won't you, will you, won't you, will you join the dance?"

Will I join the dance, or will I wander through life wondering why I don't feel better? Yes! At last I'll join the lobster quadrille, or I'll fly, or I'll stand on mountaintops and sing. Because life with God was meant to be a *joy*, not imprisonment or punishment. And just knowing that life with God is meant to be joyful may help cure me of my desire to overeat.

FOR FURTHER REFLECTION

Think about your attitude toward life. Are you joyful and full of singing and dancing, or do you have the defeated spirit of a prisoner? And how does that affect your overeating?

PRAYER

Gracious God, let me forever join Your eternal dance. Amen

Hope for the Tree

For there is hope for a tree, if it is cut down,
that it will sprout again, and that its shoots will not cease.
—Job 14:7

I will never forget growing up on the Arizona desert, where each spring was ushered in by the blooming of the saguaro cactus and ocotillo and the pungent greasewood. Greasewood is a relative of beets and spinach, but with its dull gray bark and thorny branches it bears little resemblance to its edible cousins. Unlike beets or other members of its family, the greasewood never really dies. New shoots come from around its ancient rootstalk, and biologists believe that some greasewood plants are several thousand years old.

When I went to my school reunion the desert was at its spring loveliest. Paloverde trees were heavy with lacy yellow blossoms. Saguaros bore crowns of pure white flowers. Graceful cactus wrens swooped in and out of nests, feeding their young. And the homely greasewood tree stood proud to remind me that even a soul dead in its sin, a lifeless personality that looks to food for solace and joy can be resurrected. The hard part is being cut down so I can sprout new life.

FOR FURTHER REFLECTION

Plant something today, either in your garden or in a pot in your kitchen. Each time you feel like nibbling, care for the plant instead: water it, loosen the soil, or even sing to it. Let it be a symbol to you of God's promise to nurture you and to give you new life.

PRAYER

Give me new life today, Lord. Amen

Control

*For this very reason, you must make every effort to support
your faith with goodness, and goodness with knowledge,
and knowledge with self-control, and self-control with endurance,
and endurance with godliness, and godliness with
mutual affection, and mutual affection with love.*
—2 Peter 1:5-7

We've all known "control freaks" who try to manage and manipulate others. Their opposites are people who act like seaweed being tossed around in a stormy sea, just "going with the flow."

And both the control freaks and the "seaweed" folks are inclined to have eating problems, either overeating or going into anorexia: the controllers to reassure themselves that they're in control, and the weaker people to feel stronger.

Somewhere in the middle is an individual who prefers not to control or be controlled, a man or woman who is self-directed and who looks only to Jesus as master. People who manage their own lives that way are less likely to have any serious eating problems. This person lives *intentionally*, relying neither on old habits nor on skewed emotional needs; he or she has added to goodness, knowledge; and to knowledge, self-control; and to self-control, perseverance.

A children's hymn called "The Saints of God" ends each verse with, "And I want to be one, too." Yeah.

FOR FURTHER REFLECTION
When you find yourself in a difficult position where you are unable to control your circumstances, do you know how to control your reactions to those circumstances?

PRAYER
O Master, let me follow You. Amen

Blackbirds

But ask the animals, and they will teach you;
the birds of the air, and they will tell you . . .

—Job 12:7

When I stepped out on my front porch this morning, the slope in front of my house was covered with blackbirds, eating the bright red berries on my cotoneaster. The slope was a mound of moving black feathers, and the birds stayed about forty minutes. When they finally rose in a cloud of black, swooping back and forth and finally flying away, not a single red berry was left.

Birds know exactly how much they need to eat. Most varieties have to consume their own weight daily, just to stay alive. In fact, most animals—birds, beasts, and fish—usually eat only what they need. They don't find something they like and stuff themselves with it as humans do; they just add on weight in the summer to get them through the winter. Usually the only creatures that overeat are pets that live with indulgent human beings, or tamed squirrels and pigeons in parks.

If human influence can make an animal overeat, what does that say about us?

FOR FURTHER REFLECTION

1. Have you come to believe that you need to eat as much as you do?
2. What can you do to help yourself get in touch with the truth about what your body requires to be well nourished?

PRAYER

Lord, You gave the animals instincts to eat
the right amount and the correct diet.
But You gave me intelligence and consciousness
instead. Help me to use them. Amen

Another Choice

Go your way, eat the fat and drink sweet wine
and send portions of them to those for whom nothing
is prepared, for this day is holy to our Lord;
and do not be grieved, for the joy of the Lord is your strength.
                                                    —Nehemiah 8:10

While I was writing this book, we traveled through seven southern states. At just about every meal, I had to have a "doggy bag" because southern portions are so large. In Arkansas we found a wonderful café that listed "vegetables" you could choose with the main dish. Some, like collard greens and squash, were really vegetables; others, such as macaroni and cheese or baked beans belonged in a different category.

When I chose pot roast from the menu, with potatoes, carrots, and onions, I asked for a salad and declined anything else. "But you still have another choice!" the waiter exclaimed. I smiled and declined, so he left, shaking his head.

Now that I'm home, his words have stayed with me, and I've realized that even though I always have another choice (or three or five), I don't have to take it. I can decline any number of offerings. And that realization is freeing. The refrigerator and cupboards may be full of food, but that doesn't mean I have to eat it.

FOR FURTHER REFLECTION

1. *Do you give in when you have too many choices?*
2. *How can you resist this kind of temptation?*
3. *How can you prepare to make food choices when you're confronted with them?*

PRAYER

Remind me when I've had enough, God,
and remind me that I can choose to decline. Amen

Bread and Salt

He said to his daughters, "Where is he?
Why did you leave the man? Invite him to break bread."
—Exodus 2:20

Bread is a staple of every diet in every culture: flatbröd, tortilla, injera, baba, pita, and chapalas are among the many ethnic breads of the world. And salt is a basic necessity to human electrolyte balance.

In Arab tradition, you eat bread and salt with another person to establish friendship. Bread and salt are part of a traditional Russian ceremony of welcome. At a Polish wedding reception, the parents of the bride and groom greet the newly married couple with bread lightly sprinkled with salt. Guests in Ukraine are offered a circular bread (*klib*) and a mold of salt (*sil*) on an embroidered ceremonial cloth, and accompanied with the words, "With this bread and salt we greet you." Jewish tradition urges bringing bread and salt to people who move into a new home. In so doing, tradition says, the people can sustain themselves.

Although I don't want a dull diet, I *could* forego cannelloni, pecan-crusted chicken, and black bottom pie. After all, what I asked God for was my daily bread.

FOR FURTHER REFLECTION

1. Are you skipping the ceremonial part of your meals?
2. Does your dinner hour contain elements of tradition and sharing?
3. Would considering the basic components of your meals simplify them?

PRAYER

Thank you, God, for bread and salt
and milk and honey. Help me to eat simply. Amen

Samurai

There is none like God, O Jeshurun,
who rides through the heavens to your help,
majestic through the skies.

—Deuteronomy 33:26

Medieval Japanese texts speak of *kyûba no michi* ("the way of horse and bow"), a description of the life of a samurai warrior. These men, to whom family honor was ultimately important, managed feudal lands; but their major occupations were war and training for war.

Whether with a bow and arrow, a musket, or an Uzi, to spend life preparing for battle is the world's way, not God's. "He subdues the ancient gods, shatters the forces of old; he drove out the enemy before you . . . Happy are you, O Israel! Who is like you, a people saved by the Lord, the shield of your help, and the sword of your triumph! Your enemies shall come fawning to you, and you shall tread on their backs."

For me to go to war with my nibbling habit wouldn't be the way of the Lord, either. I don't need to fight—in fact, the harder I battle, the more likely I am to fail. Only when I admit my helplessness and my dependence on God can I be victorious. No samurai needed here; God is the warrior.

FOR FURTHER REFLECTION

1. *Do you think you have to fight the food battle alone?*
2. *Are you allowing God to work in all your life?*
3. *Do you think your nibbling is too small a problem to take to God?*

PRAYER

To the only God our Savior be glory,
majesty, power, and victory. Amen

Desert Wind

Then the Lord answered Job out of the whirlwind.
—Job 38:1

On the desert where I grew up, the tall saguaro cactus lift their arms as if praising God, and the warm, dry air creates little whirlwinds of dust everywhere. After my Sunday School teacher introduced me to the Book of Job—I was about ten—I started chasing those "dust devils" to see if I could hear God talking. I never did, although once while running after the whirlwind I stumbled over a young fox, who yipped as we collided.

We all chase whirlwinds or look for handwriting on walls. Even after asking God for guidance, we aren't willing to believe that casual words spoken by a friend could be that guidance. The signs are present, but unless they come from the hot desert wind or the mouth of a donkey, we don't want to believe them.

I don't have to be a storm chaser to hear God's voice. In fact, God could be speaking through my little dog, who is whining right this minute to go for a long walk. Maybe a stroll through the hills would be better than staying home with my nachos.

FOR FURTHER REFLECTION

Think about the ways God may speak to you and guide you: first through the Bible, then through other spiritual reading, sermons, and the words of friends. What is the message God is sending you today?

PRAYER

Grant me, gracious Lord,
the ability to hear You when You speak. Amen

Shepherd's Oil

You prepare a table before me
in the presence of my enemies;
you anoint my head with oil; my cup overflows.
—Psalm 23:5

When I was in Israel, I took a photograph of a young boy with a flock of sheep, grazing only a few feet from a lush wheat field. In Middle Eastern countries, sheep growers don't fence their animals in a field full of green grass. They move their flocks from place to place and always put someone with the sheep, both to protect them from predators and to keep them out of juicy wheat fields.

When the sheep come in for the night, the shepherds run them under a stream of water to wash their fleece, and then each sheep gets a dollop of oil on its head, to keep out mites and to lubricate the sheep's face. Although sheep have lanolin glands, their faces can become dry and their noses chapped.

Today as I edged toward a box of cookies, I felt something like a dollop of oil, an anointing, to remind me that food isn't what I'm hungry for.

FOR FURTHER REFLECTION

Today, think about your personal spiritual journey, then journal a page about the times in your life when God has anointed your mind or spirit or emotions.

PRAYER

You are my Shepherd, Lord God.
Keep splashing me with Your anointing. Amen

Can of Worms

Truly, your God is God of gods and
Lord of kings and a revealer of mysteries,
for you have been able to reveal this mystery!
—Daniel 2:47

I was sitting on the front porch with my Bible when a neighbor passed by. "Hey, you're opening a can of worms by reading that book," he said, laughing. He waved and went on, but I sat for a long time, staring at the street, thinking about what he said.

Life would be a lot simpler without God. I could do what I wanted, go where I liked, or indulge my feelings. I could yell at people I'm mad at, laugh out loud at anyone I consider stupid, and above all, I could eat what I want, when I want.

Yes, life without God would be simple and natural. The only problem is, life without God is no life at all.

And besides, the can of worms is already open. I've read the book—and believe me, I've peeked at the ending—and experienced God's presence in my life. I can't pretend now that I don't know the rules or the promise. So I guess if God wants me to stop nibbling, I better pay attention.

FOR FURTHER REFLECTION

1. *How would you behave without the Bible to guide you?*
2. *What would you be without God in your life?*
3. *Which life would you prefer?*

PRAYER

Thank you, God, for being in my life
and constantly revealing Yourself to me. Amen

No Turning Back

But the one who endures
to the end will be saved.

—Matthew 10:22

Most people have no trouble starting something like exercise or a diet or journaling. At the New Year or during Lent, everybody begins a new program with the best of intentions . . . but soon, most of those people have fallen by the wayside. The demands of daily life sabotage our plans, or temptation becomes too great. Only a really determined person can endure to the end.

I've started a hundred good diets and food plans and eating schemes. And I've always sunk slowly back into my old habits, eventually giving up. But this time, something is different. This time, I've made God part of my effort.

This time, I have to admit that I'm pretty helpless where nibbling and overeating and bad eating are concerned. I also have to *believe* that God wants to help me overcome that helplessness. With God's help, I can do anything. I don't have to just grit my teeth and stick to my resolve; what I have to set my mind to is God's loving presence in my life.

FOR FURTHER REFLECTION

How can you prepare for the next time you feel your resolve weakening?

PRAYER

Dear Lord, take my eating, and temper it
with Your beautiful spirit. Amen

References

I will do whatever you ask in my name,
so that the Father may be glorified in the Son.

—John 14:13

Most publishers are so inundated with unsolicited manuscripts that they don't read all of them. You have to query an editor, and your query has to be convincing. So I told a new writer to send a proposal for her book to my publisher—and say I recommended it. My name isn't magic, but its influence did get the writer's work a reading. Eventually the publisher accepted it. Without the name of someone she knew commending the book, the editor might never have seen the manuscript.

The name of Jesus carries a lot more weight in the spiritual world than mine does with a publisher. Now *there's* a name worth using in high places. So when I say, "Help me with my eating, God," I can add "in Jesus' name."

FOR FURTHER REFLECTION

Dietrich Bonhoeffer, the German theologian, said, "The word God means nothing; the name *of God means everything." Take some time alone today, and think about the way you use Jesus' powerful name. Ask one more time for help with your eating. And do it in the name of Jesus.*

PRAYER

Help me with my eating problem, God.
In Jesus' name. Amen

Peaceful Slumber

I will both lie down and sleep in peace;
for you alone, O Lord, make me lie down in safety.
—Psalm 4:8

It's amazing how quickly I turn to doughnuts to wake me up after getting too little sleep, or to macaroni and cheese and chocolate milk, or maybe even a pint of ice cream as a reward when I've been working late. Not only are these bad food choices, but eating so late at night makes it difficult to get to sleep, which then makes it difficult to wake up on time. And as another day dawns, once again I find myself rushing out the door and grabbing a doughnut or a bagel slathered with cream cheese on my way to work.

That's no way to start the day. I need to give my body a fighting chance to do its best work. Eating too late to let my food be digested; not getting enough sleep; and loading up on fat and sugar to "revive" me is a recipe for very bad health.

I need to make getting a good night's sleep a priority in my life.

FOR FURTHER REFLECTION

Take note of how your eating patterns relate to your sleeping patterns. If getting too little sleep or staying up too late leads to rash meal choices, do you need to change your schedule?

PRAYER

Heavenly Father, let me rest body and soul in You. Amen

Invitation

While they were eating, Jesus took a loaf of bread,
and after blessing it he broke it, gave it to the disciples,
and said, "Take, eat; this is my body."
—Matthew 26:26

Here's the paradox: Jesus says to me, "Take, eat," but my common sense tells me to stop eating. I can't take what Jesus offers if I'm already taking in too much of everything else. So maybe part of the message is that I need to be prepared to accept what He is giving me instead of filling up on harmful thoughts, activities, and food.

He says if I take what He offers, I will have food for my body and soul. And He also says not to worry about what I eat or drink but to seek first the kingdom of God and everything I need will be given to me. Imagine that. Eating without worrying. Being filled with every good thing, so that saying "no" to unhealthy habits comes easily.

Tonight, when that late-evening snack attack comes over me, I'm going to eat from the Bread of Life, God's Word. And maybe temptation will go on the run.

FOR FURTHER REFLECTION

Find a quiet place to relax for a few minutes. Take a deep breath. Take another. Refer to a favorite Bible verse concerning stillness or choose a less familiar one using the concordance. When you are at peace, ask yourself if you feel the need to eat or if you already feel full.

PRAYER

Humbly, I come before You, Lord Jesus,
filled with gratitude for Your tender mercies. Amen

The Wedding Supper

Let us rejoice and exult and give him the glory,
for the marriage of the Lamb has come,
and his bride has made herself ready.

—Revelation 19:7

I once had a kitten who, I knew, would become the greatest hunter cat in the state. He pounced on everything that moved, and quickly subdued any kind of ball or string or spool. Everybody enjoyed watching him play, but we also knew that his play was rehearsal for the day he'd head into the fields, stalking mice and voles. He had to play as a rehearsal for hunting.

I think eating on earth is like that kitten's activities. Just play, just rehearsal for the day we sit in heaven at the wedding supper of the Lamb. If I can learn to eat here on earth, eat properly with great enjoyment but without stuffing or starving myself, I'll be ready for that feast.

My rehearsal has begun. I'll eat of the grain God brings from the earth, from the fruit of the vines, from the many wonderful, nourishing foods God has put here. And one day I can attend that great supper where Christ is the Bridegroom and I am part of his linen-clad Bride, the Church.

FOR FURTHER REFLECTION

1. *Is managing your eating hard work?*
2. *Would it be easier if you took a more playful approach to it?*

PRAYER

Lord Christ, I long to spend eternity with You.
Keep me close to You and guide me to the banquet. Amen

In the Fire

But I see four men unbound,
walking in the middle of the fire . . .
and the fourth has the appearance of a god.
—Daniel 3:25

Nebuchadnezzar had his musicians sound the horn, pipe, lyre, trigon, har, and drum, but Shadrach, Meshach, and Abednego refused to bow down. So he ordered the fiery furnace to be heated up to seven times its normal temperature, and then threw them in. They walked in the fire, unharmed, and a fourth man walked beside them, one with the appearance of God. That fourth man in the furnace, the one with the shining, celestial appearance, the one who whispered "I'm here! Keep walking!" to Shadrach, Meshach, and Abednego, is the same one who walks with me every time I get near the heat.

For me, the furnace is in the refrigerator, the cupboards, and the breadbox. I may not be in immediate danger of physical death from overeating, but in addition to the long-term physical harm I'm doing, I'm placing my emotional and spiritual life at risk.

When my struggle with food heats up, I need to remember that God is in the fire with me, saying "I'm here! Keep walking! I can bring you through this if you trust me."

FOR FURTHER REFLECTION

1. *Are you aware of God's presence when you're tempted to eat unhealthily?*
2. *Do you feel as if you're walking in "the fiery furnace"?*
3. *Can you believe God will deliver you?*

PRAYER

I'm afraid of the fire, God,
afraid of being consumed by my overeating.
Hold my hand as we walk through the fire together. Amen

A New Spirit

Create in me a clean heart, O God,
and put a new and right spirit within me.

—Psalm 51:10

When I write a mystery novel, I try to hide the conclusion. After all, I want my readers to be surprised by the outcome. But God reveals the plan for every new chapter in our lives. God sends prophets to tell us every time something is about to occur. We are called to be on the alert for the marvelous things God has in store for us.

In spring, everything is new. The pale green leaf buds on our Oregon white alder trees let me know that spring is here. The swallows that nested again this year under the eaves of our garage—and swoop down on my little dog—say summer isn't far behind. And the grandeur of the night sky tells me that God is always doing a new thing somewhere, creating a new star, or even letting a new galaxy burst into being.

God's doing a new thing in my life, too. He's giving me a new spirit, showing me that my overeating can be a thing of the past, and He's turning me into a stronger, happier person.

FOR FURTHER REFLECTION

Today, take a look at the new thing God is doing in your life, and make a list of the changes you and God have already made.

PRAYER

Dear God, give me eyes, ears, and a heart
that can perceive the new spirit
You are creating in me. Amen

A New Way

The spirit of the Lord speaks through me,
his word is upon my tongue.

—2 Samuel 23:1, 2

I'd like to put into practice all the lessons I've learned in my journey toward healthier eating. Here's my plan: First, I'm going to continue journaling my thoughts about eating—if not every day, then at least several times a week. I'm also going to keep a record of everything I eat, every day, just to make me aware of my eating habits.

Secondly, every time I crave something unhealthy, I'm going to divert my attention for at least twenty minutes. I'll take the dog for a walk; or I'll work on my photo albums; or I'll play the piano. I'm going to respond to all my "triggers" with non-eating activities.

I'm also going to add more ceremony to my meals. No matter how busy I am, I'll quit lunching at my desk. I won't have dinner while watching television. I'll use my best dishes every night, and light candles on the table. When my grandchildren are visiting, I'll show them the beauty of shared sit-down meals.

Finally, I'm going to remember to think about the food I'm eating without being hypercritical of myself or my past mistakes. God has put a new spirit in me and He is about to do a new thing in my life, so there's no reason for me to be bogged down by the past, or to feel defeated if I stray from my plan. After all, it's God's plan that counts.

FOR FURTHER REFLECTION

Prayerfully devise a plan that will work for you. And remember, every *moment* brings a new opportunity to let God work in you, so don't ever let yourself feel like a failure.

PRAYER

Dear God, guide me as I seek to follow Jesus in every way. Amen

Notes

Notes

Notes

Notes

Notes

Notes

Notes

Notes

Notes

Notes

Notes

Notes

Notes

Notes

Notes

Notes

Notes

Notes